SPIRITUS
SANCTUS
The Holy Spirit

DR. EMMANUEL OSEI-ACHEAMPONG

SPIRITUS SANCTUS

The Holy Spirit

DR. EMMANUEL OSEI-ACHEAMPONG

WESTBOW®
PRESS
A DIVISION OF THOMAS NELSON
& ZONDERVAN

WestBow Press books may be ordered through booksellers or by contacting:

WestBow Press
A Division of Thomas Nelson & Zondervan
1663 Liberty Drive
Bloomington, IN 47403
www.westbowpress.com
1 (866) 928-1240

ISBN: 978-1-4908-2925-8 (sc)
ISBN: 978-1-4908-2923-4 (hc)
ISBN: 978-1-4908-2924-1 (e)

Library of Congress Control Number: 2014904472

Printed in the United States of America.

WestBow Press rev. date: 4/10/2014

Contents

Dedicated with love to
my beloved father,
Osofo Francis Kwabena Acheampong,
and my beloved mother,
Elizabeth Afia Dansowa Acheampong.

Dear Friend,

Prepare your mind, heart, and soul. You are about to enter the ultimate *Power* Zone of Jehovah's ultimate authority. To understand the power, which is ready to be released in you in the name of the Lord, Jesus Christ, please carefully read the preface and the introduction.

God is already doing something wonderful in your life, and He is about to move you to a higher level of anointing. The Holy Spirit's anointing power is ready to increase your knowledge, your power, your zeal, and your desire to be on fire for Jesus.

Be a kingdom-of-God builder.

—Dr. Emmanuel Osei-Acheampong
Servant of the Lord Jesus Christ

Acknowledgments

Every book is a team effort. This book is expressly so!

Special thanksgiving to the Team Leader, the Holy Spirit of God who inspired the writing of this book, to the praise and glory of God in the name of our Lord and Savior Jesus Christ.

Special thanks also to the faithful administrative team who labored tirelessly to put it together. Your labor of love is never in vain in the Lord, who shall continue to shower you with His perfect blessings.

And all things, whatever you ask in prayer,
believing, you will receive.
—Matthew 21:22

Preface

One divine person, which the present-day Christian may be most unsure of or is confused about, is the Holy Spirit. Many teachings abound about the Holy Spirit by various theological proponents. The Lord has inspired me to write this book to elucidate on the Holy Spirit because the Holy Spirit is the most important divine person needed for the Christian life. In John 4:23–24, Jesus Christ teaching the woman at the well stated categorically and emphatically, "But the hour is coming, and now is, when the true worshippers will worship the Father in spirit and in truth, for the Father is seeking such to worship Him. God is Spirit and those who worship Him must worship Him in spirit and in truth."

In John 3:3, while teaching Nicodemus, Jesus again commanded, "Most assuredly I say to you, unless one is born again, he cannot see the Kingdom of God." In verse 5, it says, "Most assuredly I say to you, unless one is born of water and of the Spirit, he cannot enter the kingdom of God."

God desires true worshippers to worship Him in Spirit and mandates that everyone has to be born again of the Spirit to enter the kingdom of God. Therefore, it is necessary that a Christian must understand all he or she can about the Holy Spirit in order to eliminate confusion. The good news is that the Holy Spirit Himself will lead you into all truth, and it is the will of God to fill you with the Holy Spirit.

In the following pages, the author will endeavor to answer very basic questions about the Holy Spirit, such as, "Who is the Holy Spirit?," "Where does He come from?," "Where does He live?," "When He comes, how does He work?," and other important aspects of the Holy Spirit that everyone must know in order to be a well-rounded, rooted, and grounded Christian.

Inspired by the Holy Spirit, the author hopes this book will help and inspire you to the glory of God.

I pray that the Lord Jesus Christ opens your understanding to receive that which is holy, which is the word of God.

The grace of our Lord, Jesus Christ and the love of God be with you as you read.

Introduction

The author, by the grace of God, is filled and baptized with the Holy Spirit. He is anointed with the gifts to manifest and demonstrate the power of the Holy Spirit in the name of the Lord, Jesus Christ, and to the ultimate glory of God. He appreciates theology and "sound doctrine."

However, this book is not a theological treatise, nor is it a doctrinal exposition. This book is intended to *free your mind, body,* and *soul* from putting the *almighty God* in a box of rules and regulations of creeds, dogmas, religions, articles, and statements of faith, affirmations, denominations, organizational sectarianism, and name-brand ministries with all its paraphernalia. God, our Lord, Jesus Christ, the Holy Spirit, time, and recovered truth, knowledge, and understanding have proven to be good and now need to coalesce to inspire the "*forward movement*" of God's people with the *Holy Spirit movement.*

The Holy Spirit has three major purposes:

1. To foster love in and unite all God's people in the perfect Son of God, the Lord Jesus Christ. The Holy Spirit accomplishes this by producing the fruit of the Spirit in the believer.
2. To empower believers to fulfill the great commission, which is to make disciples of all nations. This is also accomplished by impartation and activation of the gifts of

the Spirit to anoint the believer for evangelism. Acts 1:8 says, "But you shall receive power when the Holy Spirit has come upon you; and you shall be witnesses to me in Jerusalem, and in all Judea and Samaria, and to the end of the earth."

3. To equip and mature believers for the work, defense and edification of the ministry. The Holy Spirit accomplishes these in three major areas.

   (a) By the fivefold ministry offices. Ephesians 4:11–12: "And He Himself gave some to be apostles, some prophets, some evangelists, some pastors, and teachers for the equipping of the saints for the work of ministry, for the edifying of the body of Christ."

   (b) Regeneration and transformation. Romans 12:2: "And do not be conformed to this world, but be transformed by the renewing of your mind, that you may prove what is that good and acceptable and perfect will of God." Colossians 3:17: "And whatever you do in word or deed, do all in the name of the Lord Jesus, giving thanks to God the Father through Him."

   (c) By causing growth and maturity in the believer in your language, attitude, behavior and character. Colossians 4:6: "Let your speech always be with grace, seasoned with salt, that you may know how you ought to answer each one." Second Corinthians 6:3: "We give no offense in anything, that our ministry may not be blamed." Colossians 3:17: "And whatever you do in word or deed, do all in the name of the Lord Jesus, Giving thanks to God the Father through Him." Colossians 3:23: "And whatever you do, do it heartily, as to the Lord and not to men." Colossians 3:12–14: "Therefore, as the elect of God, holy and beloved, put on tender mercies, kindness, humility, meekness, long-suffering; bearing with one another, and forgiving one another, if anyone has a complaint against another; even as Christ forgave you, so you also must do. But above all these things put on love, which is the bond of perfection."

This book is about revealing, teaching, and opening up of your mind, heart, and soul to God's mighty gift to you, the Holy Spirit of God. It is to help you to *leave behind* the limitations of frustrating *powerless Christianity*, holier-than-thou Christianity, and judgmental and condemnatory Christianity, and move you to the higher realm of the Gospel of reconciliation, sanctification, unity of the brethren, and to the overcoming and conquering power level of the supernatural with the *unlimited power* of the Holy Spirit awaiting every believer of the Lord Jesus Christ. It is to propel you to the higher maturity level of perfect love, which casts out fear.

This book is to help you *move away* from a stagnant and despairing Christianity to a dynamic full of faith, love, prayer, and Holy Spirit power and a can-do-all-things-through-Christ type of anointed Christianity.

This book will take you to the experiential realm of the Holy Spirit, and when you experience the Holy Spirit, there shall be a spiritual revival in your own soul and life in general. This book will reawaken your zeal and take you back to your first love, when you first believed in the Lord, Jesus Christ.

Do you know what your spiritual gifts are? This book reveals the many spiritual gifts available to every believer. Every Holy

Spirit-baptized believer receives one or more gifts from God. This book will help you to know more about your gifts and how to use them.

Spiritus Sanctus will help stir up that Holy Spirit gift in you, stir up your anointing, and stir up your zeal with knowledge to work for the Lord. This book will reveal many other gifts of the Holy Spirit, which the majority of believers have not paid enough attention to, hence, the apparent semblance of weakness and powerlessness in Christianity today.

Why be a "lame-duck Christian" when the Lord says, "You shall receive power after that the Holy Spirit is come upon you …" (Act 1:8). You can be *endued* with *power* today and rise up and let your *power light* (you are the light of the world) shine everywhere to every creature in the name of Jesus and to the ultimate glory of God.

Remember, when you are filled with the Holy Spirit, you can boldly say, "Greater is He that is in me than He that is in the world" (1 John 4:4). Now unto Him who is able to keep you from falling and to present you faultless before the presence of His glory with exceeding joy, to the only wise God our Savior, be glory and majesty, dominion and power, both now and forever in the name of our Lord, Jesus Christ.

CHAPTER 1

Marvel Not

In a survey conducted by the author, three thousand Christians of all ages and of diverse denominations were asked two questions:

1. Who is the Holy Spirit?
2. Where does He live?

The results added fuel to the author's fire in his desire to share the knowledge in this book. An additional three thousand non-Christians of all ages were asked the same questions, and the answers were, sadly, as expected.

Among Christians, 58 percent were unable to say exactly who the Holy Spirit is. It became more ambiguous when they put Him in gender. Sixteen percent called Him "She," 35 percent called Him "it," and the rest called Him "He." Twenty percent of Christians interviewed had partially correct answers, and only 22 percent had exact answers regarding the second question, "Where does He live?" It became obvious that many of the Christians interviewed read the Bible with some misunderstanding and may be confused by diverse doctrines.

Interestingly, some Christians made a statement like, "The Holy Spirit is the one who gives life, so He lives in everything that has life." (The author does not believe that snakes or witches are filled with the Holy Spirit.)

Of the three thousand non-Christians interviewed, 10 percent were able to say who He is, and 2 percent were able to say where He lives. This 2 percent turned out to be backsliders. Ninety percent of all non-Christians were unhappy with the questions, and some said, "I don't know, and I don't want to know, thank you." But El Shaddai, God almighty, wants us to know, honor, and respect Him as revealed in Psalm 46:10, which commands, "Be still and know that I am God," and Ecclesiastes 12:13, which says, "Let us hear the conclusion of the whole matter: Fear God and keep His commandments, for this is the whole duty of man."

The Lord, Jesus told the Samaritan woman at the well, "You worship what you do not know, we know what we worship." It is clear and obvious that many people want to know who or what they worship.

God alone is God, so it is good to know Him and worship Him in Spirit and in truth. In the pages of this book, the Holy Spirit has inspired the author to give very precise answers to these rather fundamental questions of the Christian life. Praise God for His precision and grace. I believe that when you understand these fundamental questions about the Holy Spirit, the confusion about Him will be dramatically diminished. Your love of God will increase exponentially with your zeal to be on fire for Jesus. Your anointing will soar like an eagle, and your ministry will blossom like a garden of roses.

May the Lord bless everyone who reads this book and keep the anointing flowing through you in the name of Jesus Christ, our Lord and Savior.

I pray that the Holy Spirit will lead you into all truth, and that you may know there is a length, breadth, and height to the Scriptures (Ephesians 3:18), there are deeper depths and higher heights in the word of God.

Blessed are the pure in heart, for they shall see God.
—Matthew 5:8

CHAPTER 2

Who?

I recently witnessed a very powerful and highly educational incident at a children's party.

A charming, five-year-old boy (whom we shall call Enoch) was having a discourse with a six-year-old boy (whom we shall call Thomas) in the dining room full of goodies for kids. Enoch had just tasted honey and was busy licking his right index finger.

Thomas asked, "What's that on your finger, and why are you licking it?"

Enoch answered, "It's finger-licking good. It's honey."

Thomas asked, "What is it?"

Enoch answered, "Honey. My daddy says it's good for the body. It will make you strong"—he flexed his muscles—"and it's sweet."

Thomas said, "Yuk. That's poison. How do you know it's sweet?"

Enoch answered, "Here, taste it." He squirted honey onto his finger and smeared it on Thomas's lips.

Thomas said, "Mmm! Well, it is like sugar. It's sweet. It's like Mom's syrup. Yeah, it's sweet!"

Enoch said, "Yes, that's honey. Sweeter than sugar and syrup. I told you it is honey. Now eat it, and be strong like me."

They laughed and began sharing the honey with other kids having fun at the party. The Holy Spirit taught me through this beautiful incident that some people, believers as well as unbelievers, are like Thomas, and some are believers like Enoch. I learned two powerful lessons.

1. Enoch knew what honey was, and though Thomas called it poison, Enoch was not moved or terrified. Enoch knew what he was eating and could not be shaken or confused. Enoch was even so kind and eager to share what he had that he actually caused Thomas to taste and believe.

    Enoch is the type of believer or minister of the Lord Jesus Christ who has tasted of the Spirit, is full of the Holy Spirit, and is constantly praying for other believers and seekers to believe in the Lord Jesus and be filled with the Holy Spirit. He also practices personal evangelism by sharing the gospel of the Lord Jesus Christ.

2. Thomas did not know what honey was. He called it poison, was afraid of it, and would not taste it until forced. Thomas is a type of believer or unbeliever who is not filled with the Holy Spirit. His or her mind is filled with doubt.

You try to figure out who the Holy Spirit is. You see people under the anointing and conclude they are abnormal because that is not how you worship God. But once Thomas tasted the honey, he was not poisoned and became excited like Enoch.

My friend, taste of the Holy Spirit, and you'll never be the same again. You'll become a true believer and will be on fire for Jesus.

Having learned the powerful lessons above, let us now find out the following:

Who is the Holy Spirit?

1. He is the Spirit of God.

The following Scriptures make this answer very clear.

"But the hour is coming, and now is, when the true worshippers will worship the Father in Spirit and in Truth; for the Father is seeking such to worship Him" (John 4:23).

"God is a Spirit, and those who worship Him must worship in Spirit and in Truth" (John 4:24).

The Holy Bible explicitly declares that God is Spirit. Therefore, the Holy Spirit is the Spirit of God. Let us study a few more clarifying Scriptures.

> And it shall come to pass afterward that I will pour out my Spirit on all flesh; your sons and your daughters shall prophesy, your old men shall dream dreams, your young men shall see visions; and also on my menservants and on my maidservants I will pour out my Spirit in those days. (Joel 2:28–29)

Here God unilaterally declares, "I will pour out my Holy Spirit on all flesh."

"My Spirit shall not always strive with man forever, for he is indeed flesh" (Genesis 6:3).

"I will pour out my Spirit on you; I will make my word known to you" (Proverbs 1:23).

"I will pour out my Spirit on your descendants" (Isaiah 44:3).

We read in the above and throughout the Bible that when God says, "My Spirit," it is understood to refer to the Holy Spirit. Therefore, the author concludes that the Holy Spirit is the Spirit of God.

2. He is God.

> But Peter said, "Ananias, why has Satan filled your heart to lie to the Holy Spirit and keep back part of the price of the land for yourself? While it remained, was it not your own? And after it was sold, was it not in your own control? Why have you conceived this thing in your heart? You have not lied to men but to God." (Acts 5:3–4)

This passage reveals authentically that the apostle Peter, who recently experienced the special outpouring of the Holy Spirit during Pentecost, is saying to Ananias and his wife, "You have lied to the Holy Spirit in me, and the Holy Spirit in me is God."

"God was in Christ reconciling the world to Himself" (2 Corinthians 5:19).

This Scripture reveals that God was in Jesus Christ. However, Luke 1:35 reveals that the Holy Spirit caused Mary to conceive, thereby making the Holy Spirit the Father of Jesus. The same Scripture concludes, "That Holy One who is to be born will be called the Son of God." Therefore, the author submits that the Holy Spirit is God, who was in Christ working supernatural miracles and reconciling the world to Himself.

3. He is the Spirit of Jesus Christ.

"But you are not in the flesh but in the Spirit, if indeed the Spirit of God dwells in you. Now if anyone does not have the Spirit of Christ, he is not His" (Romans 8:9).

"God [the Spirit] was in Christ reconciling the world to Himself" (2 Corinthians 5:19).

"For I know that this will turn out for my salvation through your prayer and the supply of the Spirit of Jesus Christ" (Philippians 1:19).

The above Scriptures reveal that the Spirit of God is the Spirit of Jesus Christ. Truly Jesus is correct when He says, "I and my Father are one" (John 10:30).

This further explains the oneness of the Trinity. In all manifestations of God, He is Spirit whether by Himself as God the Father, in the form of man as seen in the Lord Jesus as God the Son, or in the believer as God the Holy Spirit. Galatians 4:6 reveals that "And because you are sons, God has sent the spirit of His Son [Jesus Christ] into your hearts, crying, 'Abba, Father!'" He is Spirit and He is God at all times.

Henceforth, the world ought to reverence the Holy Spirit because now it knows that the Holy Spirit is the Spirit of the Lord, Jesus Christ, the Spirit of God, and is God.

Trust in the LORD with all your heart, and lean not on your own understanding. In all your ways acknowledge Him, and He shall direct your paths.
—Proverbs 3:5–6

CHAPTER 3

Where?

In one of my blessed travels, my journey took me to Geneva, Switzerland. Like most visitors to other towns, cities, states, and continents, I did not know how to find my way around like the residents. And as most experienced travelers do, I asked several times for directions to my various destinations whenever the city map could not help me. Almost in all circumstances, the people asked me a question as soon as I finished asking for directions. Most asked, "Where are you from?" Of course I smiled and answered. Then they answered my question.

Dear reader, I believe you have traveled to some other town, city, state, or continent and have spoken to the local people in the market or malls, and some of the locals have asked you, "Where are you from?"

I recently traveled to the beautiful island of the Bahamas. On arrival, I requested the hotel-courtesy bus driver to assist me loading my baggage on the bus and the first thing he asked was, "Where are you from?"

In my quest to learn more about why people are preoccupied with the question "Where are you from?" which is, "Where do you come from?" I spoke to a university sociology professor friend of mine about it. He smiled, and though he confessed he never gave much thought to it, he admitted it has happened to him several times in his travels around the world. Here are some of the thoughts the professor shared with me.

a. There is something about a stranger in a local place that arouses curiosity.
b. The local people know their way around and tend not to ask for directions.
c. The language difference (and of course the color/ nationality difference) makes people inquisitive.
d. Most of the time, the accent difference will trigger the question.
e. The mood of the visitor, personality, affability, courteous mannerisms, and general positive attitudes are all factors that can trigger the same question.

The Lord, Jesus appears to be a stranger among us. He knew us, but we did not know Him. He came to His own, but His own received Him not. And many times, like a stranger as He appeared to them, the people asked Him several questions. So I am not surprised that someone at some point asked Him, "Where do you come from?" And so He answered in John 6:38 "I have come down from heaven."

In fact, there was a very heated argument over where the Lord Jesus comes from. Some supposed in their natural mind that He is from Nazareth. Indeed one of His early disciples, Nathaniel, spoke for the skeptics when he said, "Can anything good come out of Nazareth?" (John 1:46). So the question of where Jesus comes from was not only intriguing to them but an enigma. Here is a Nazarene who is despised but is working miracles the Bethany rabbi, the Jerusalem high priest and the

Galilee Pharisee all together had never seen and could not perceive or perform. They argued about "Whence" Jesus comes (i.e., where Jesus comes from) in that awful heated disputation in John 7:25–30: "Then some of them from Jerusalem said, 'Is this not He whom they seek to kill? But look! He speaks boldly, and they say nothing to Him. Do the rulers know indeed that this is truly the Christ? However, we know where this Man is from; but when the Christ comes, no one knows where He is from.' Then Jesus cried out, as He taught in the temple, saying, 'You both know me, and you know where I am from; and I have not come of myself, but He who sent me is true, whom you do not know. But I know Him, for I am from Him, and He sent me.' Then they sought to take Him; but no one laid a hand on Him, because His hour had not yet come."

Here He sought to put to rest the question of where He came from. So now we know where the Lord Jesus came from and where He went back to. Heaven, of course and to the Father, which is in heaven.

Now let us put to rest the same question regarding where the Holy Spirit comes from. The Lord Jesus promised to baptize every believer with the Holy Spirit. He promised to send the Holy Spirit to believers, and that is exactly what He did in Acts 2:1–4: "Now when the day of Pentecost had fully come, they were all with one accord in one place. And suddenly there came a sound from heaven, as of a rushing mighty wind, and it filled the whole house where they were sitting. Then there appeared to them divided tongues, as of fire, and one sat upon each one of them. And they were all filled with the Holy Spirit and began to speak with other tongues, as the Spirit gave them utterance."

Where does the Holy Spirit come from?

The answer to this question is to be found in the Holy Scriptures.

a. In 1 Corinthians 2:12, the apostle Paul reveals quite clearly that, "Now we have received, not the Spirit of the world, but the Spirit who is from God, that we might know the things that have been freely given to us by God." This statement simply reveals that the Holy Spirit is from God. He is not just from heaven, but He is from God. When you know where He is coming from, then you can appreciate the power and the anointing He is bringing into your life.

b. Take a look at John 15:26, which says, "But when the Helper comes, whom I shall send to you from the Father, He will testify of me." Again, the Lord Jesus confirms that the Holy Spirit is from God, the Father who is in heaven.

c. John 14:26 says, "But the Helper, the Holy Spirit, whom the Father will send in my name, He will teach you all things that I said to you."

From above, it is easily revealed from the Holy Scriptures that the Holy Spirit comes from God the Father to the believers through Jesus Christ, our Lord and Savior.

It is a great blessing to know where the Holy Spirit is coming from. Coming from God, the Holy Spirit has all the attributes of God and the power of God. He brings these holy attributes and power to the believers. No wonder, Jesus said in John 14:12

"He who believes in me, the works that I do, he will do also and greater works than these, he will do."

He was referring to the fact that anyone who believes in Him and is filled and baptized with the same Holy Spirit that He had will be anointed and empowered in the same way as He was, to do the work that He did and even more.

For the same reason, when you are filled and baptized with the Holy Spirit, you can say greater is He that is in me than he that is in the world. So beloved, be filled with the Holy Spirit and be on fire for Jesus, building the kingdom of God.

CHAPTER 4

Why?

The lady was pushing a grocery cart with a seven-year-old girl hanging on to the cart with a big smile, obviously enjoying the ride. She seemed to know me, but I have met so many people in revivals, crusades, and church services in so many places that I confess I could not remember where and when we might have met.

Anyway, she said, "Praise the Lord," to me with a beautiful smile, and I responded, "Praise the Lord." I followed with rather obvious questions: "Why are you here, and why did you bring your beautiful daughter?"

She said, "I am in a grocery store and of course I am doing my weekly groceries for the family. I bring my daughter to train her how to do groceries so when she grows up and gets married she and her family will not live in a fast food restaurant."

"That's beautiful," I said to encourage her, announcing the completion of my own shopping, and wished her to "have a nice day."

I asked a good friend, a commercial airline pilot, "Why do you do this work?"

His answer: "It's a good profession, and besides, I love to fly and get to travel to many, many cities and countries without financial stress."

There is a beautiful young lady in the corporate world. Actually, she is the vice president of the company's human resources department. She works so hard and joyfully that I was prompted to search for some reason why. So one day I gathered the courage to ask, why do you do what you do and do it so well?

Her reply was, "I love people, and it gives me pleasure to see people make progress." Can't argue with such a virtuous goal in life.

I was in a tour group in New Orleans through the French Quarter and different parts of the city. At one point we ended up with the tour guide in the kitchen of one of the many fine restaurants to experience firsthand how the chef prepares those delicious meals. The kitchen aroma boosted my already-healthy appetite. The chef joyfully took us through all the steps to prepare jambalaya, a New Orleans specialty.

"Any questions?" the chef asked, and I asked my famous questions. "Why do you go through all this pain to cook this delicacy? And why do you seemingly enjoy cooking in a hot kitchen?"

He answered with a beautiful French accent, "I enjoy cooking, and I believe everyone deserves a fine meal. It is my desire to satisfy my customers."

The group gave him well-deserved applause, especially since each of us enjoyed a plate of his fine cooking.

This young man in his mid-thirties begins his day with his daily rituals of jogging three miles, aerobic exercises, and weight training. This exercise-freak friend of mine convinced me to do the morning jog with him. I told him I am completely rusty and calcified at the joints from neck to toe so I don't think I can run. I suggested he let me drive slowly alongside his jogging path. He objected and got me running on a cool Saturday morning. I was ready to faint at the two hundred-meter mark, when he noticed and came to help me sit down and catch my breath. After what seemed like years of rest, I gathered enough breath to tell him I'd had enough running and asked, "Why do you have to torture your body to live this simple life?"

He laughed and informed me about the health benefits of exercising the most important part of you, your physical body. He took great pains to expound on how exercising your body leads to fitness, good health, endurance, good blood circulation, loss of excess weight, alertness, improved IQ, improved personality, and self-confidence.

He added, "Your soul or spirit must be given a good and beautiful house to live in."

I am an exercise convert now and jog three miles and more and I feel good.

I am involved with an after-school program where young people who need help with homework and with subjects they are not doing well with come in. One Tuesday evening I asked a young man why he loves the program. He chuckled and said, "Well, my history has improved dramatically, and I think I am on my way to becoming a great historian. Besides, all my history homework is complete. My teacher treats me better and I think I am headed to college." I was so impressed, I gave him a bear hug and wished him success.

Why do I ask all these questions? It seems various people in different professions and endeavors know why they do what they do.

This young man has three baseball bats and will not miss a Yankee baseball game at Yankee Stadium in New York City. I asked him why he is such an avid baseball fan. He laughed and said, "Sir, when I grow up I am going to be a millionaire playing baseball. What I am doing now is finding out how to get into the baseball hall of fame." What a great vision.

One day I mustered enough courage to ask several church folks why they think one must be filled and baptized with the Holy Spirit of God. Most had one or two answers, but some simply answered, "I don't know why I must be baptized with the Holy Spirit, but I know I have great desire to be baptized with the Holy Spirit of God."

There are powerful reasons the believer must be filled and baptized with the Holy Spirit of God. God always has excellent reasons for doing what He does for those who believe and obey Him. The author will share with you some cardinal reasons you must be filled and baptized with the Holy Spirit of God. The author believes that, when you learn about the spiritual reasons, the confusion and argument about why (or why not) will simply flee with the Devil, who propagates the confusion. The author believes that when you get to know these cardinal reasons, you will cease to resist the Holy Spirit and the holy hunger, and holy desire in you to be filled and baptized with the Holy Spirit will intensify so much that you'll probably be filled and baptized with the Holy Spirit before you finish reading this book.

My prayer is for you to be filled and baptized with the Holy Spirit to receive your anointing and personal spiritual power (PSP).

Fifteen Cardinal Reasons You Must Be Baptized with the Holy Spirit

The outpouring of the Holy Spirit on the day of Pentecost on the believers to fill, baptize, and empower them to continue the work of the Lord Jesus Christ and build the kingdom of

God as started by the cornerstone, Jesus Christ, is markedly the ushering in and the definite beginning of the sixth dispensation which is classified as the dispensation of grace. It made an end of the dispensation of law (fifth dispensation) and began the sixth dispensation, which is grace. In the beginning during the first dispensation (innocence) Adam and Eve lost the God-part (Holy Spirit) of them through sin in the garden of Eden and consequently were cast out of the garden and from the presence of the Most High God. Since then every human being is born without the Holy Spirit. There are very few exceptions to this fact in the Holy Bible. The most notable exceptions:

1. John the Baptist, who was filled with the Holy Spirit in the womb of his mother, Elizabeth
2. The Holy Spirit conceived the Lord Jesus Christ in the Immaculate Conception. Nevertheless, He went through water baptism and Holy Spirit baptism to show us how God requires His children to be born again in order to worship Him in Spirit and in truth.

Now the birth of Jesus Christ was as follows: After His mother was betrothed to Joseph, before they came together, she was found with child of the Holy Spirit. Then Joseph, her husband, being a just man, and not wanting to make her a public example, was minded to put her away secretly. But while he thought about these things, behold, an angel of the Lord appeared to him in a dream, saying, Joseph, son of David, do not be afraid to take to you Mary, your wife, for that which is conceived in her is of the Holy Spirit. And she will bring forth a Son, and you shall call His name JESUS, for He will save His people from their sins. Now all this was done that it might be fulfilled which was spoken by the Lord through the prophet, saying: "Behold, a virgin shall be with child, and bear a son, and they shall call His name Immanuel," which is translated, "God with us." Then Joseph, being aroused from sleep, did as the angel of the Lord commanded him and took to him his wife, and did not know her until she had brought forth her firstborn Son. And he called His name Jesus. (Matthew 1:18–25)

Matthew 3:13–16: "Then Jesus came from Galilee to John at the Jordan to be baptized by him. And John tried to prevent Him, saying, 'I have need to be baptized by You, and are You coming to me?' But Jesus answered and said to him, 'Permit it to be so now, for thus it is fitting for us to fulfill all righteousness.' Then he allowed Him. Then Jesus, when He had been baptized, came up immediately from the water; and behold, the heavens were opened to Him, and He saw the Spirit of God descending like a dove and alighting upon Him."

In a discourse with Nicodemus recorded in John 3:6–7 of the Holy Bible, the Lord Jesus declared, "That which is born of flesh is flesh, and that which is born of Spirit is Spirit. Marvel not that I said to you, You must be born again."

What a revelation! Here the Lord Jesus confirms that man is incomplete, born of flesh and is flesh. However, God, by His grace, wants to help us become complete. God declares through His Son, the Lord Jesus Christ, that in order to receive the God part of us and become part of God's family, you and I and everybody must be born again of the Spirit of God. Hitherto, we are born of the flesh and are flesh and soul only.

Thank God that it is the will of God for you to be born again to receive the Holy Spirit to be complete. To those who believed, to them He gave power (authority) to become sons of God. A person's life is controlled according to the type of spirit that controls or leads or guides the soul. If a person is not filled with the Holy Spirit of God, an evil spirit will take over and control the soul of that person.

That is why so many children, young adults, and adults are possessed with evil spirits. This also explains why our children must be filled with the Holy Spirit. The recipients of the Holy Spirit baptism include the children as well as adults as revealed in Acts 2:39: "For the promise is to you and to your children, and to all who are afar off, as many as the Lord our God will call."

The promise is indeed for all flesh who will believe in God and His Son, Jesus Christ. To this end, let me share with you some more revealed knowledge of God about why you must be baptized with the Holy Spirit. In Matthew 6:33, Jesus graciously directs every person to "seek first the kingdom of God and His righteousness, and all these things shall be added to you."

Jesus, however, did not explain then how to seek the kingdom of God until one night when a man of the Pharisees named Nicodemus, a ruler of the Jews, came to see Jesus about how he can be born again. The teaching given to Nicodemus by Jesus that night opened a great door of understanding regarding how to seek the kingdom of God.

In John 3:3, "Jesus answered and said to him, 'Most assuredly I say to you, unless one is born again he cannot see the kingdom of God.'" When Nicodemus failed to understand this spiritual statement, Jesus explained further in John 3:5: "Jesus answered,

'Most assuredly I say to you, unless one is born of the water and of the Spirit, he cannot enter the kingdom of God.'" By these teachings, one major condition was laid for everyone seeking to enter into the kingdom of God. You must be born again of the Holy Spirit.

Combing through the Holy Bible, it came to light that there are a lot of other reasons why you must be born again of the Holy Spirit. But all of them for the sake of better understanding and quick assimilation may be grouped into fifteen cardinal reasons. Keep in mind that there are zillions of other reasons, but they all connect to fifteen cardinal reasons by careful extrapolation.

Cardinal reason one: to be one of His.

Romans 8:9 says, "But you are not in the flesh but in the Spirit, if indeed the Spirit of God dwells in you. Now if anyone does not have the Spirit of Christ, he is not His." This is an excellent time to ask yourself candidly, am I one of His? If the answer is no, please fervently pray this prayer and you'll be filled by and baptized with the Holy Spirit. "Lord Jesus I am a sinner; forgive me all my sins. I confess with my mouth and believe in my heart that you died for the forgiveness of my sins. I believe you were raised up from the dead on the third day. I humbly invite, accept and receive you as my Lord and Savior. Dear God, fill me with your Holy Spirit in the name of your Holy Son Jesus Christ. Amen."

Cardinal reason two: the Holy Spirit reveals God to the believer through Jesus Christ.

Here is the sequence of revelation. First, the Holy Spirit reveals the Lord Jesus Christ to the believer. Then the Lord

Jesus Christ reveals God to the believer as seen in the following scriptures.

In Matthew 16:13–17, the Lord, Jesus Christ, had a highly spiritual discussion with his disciples concerning, "Who do men say that I, the son of man, am?" In verse 14 some of the disciples answered that Jesus is, "John the Baptist, Elijah, Jeremiah, or one of the prophets." In verse 15 Jesus asked them, "But who do you say that I am?" In verse 16 Simon Peter answered: "You are the Christ, the son of the living God." In verse 17, Jesus answered and said to Peter, "Blessed are you, Simon Bar-Jonah, for flesh and blood have not revealed this to you but my Father, who is in heaven."

God is a Spirit and God is Holy, which is why we call the Spirit of God Holy Spirit. We see then in the above paragraph that the Holy Spirit is the one who reveals Jesus Christ to the believer. Luke 10:22 declares this principle more excellently: "All things have been delivered to me by my Father, and no one knows who the Son is but the Father, and who the Father is but the Son, and the one to whom the Son wills to reveal Him."

In this Scripture, the Lord Jesus reveals that, only God (who is spirit) can reveal the Son to the believer. He concludes that only He knows who the Father is and declared that only He can reveal God, the Father, to the believer or to whom He wills.

The author concludes, that without the Holy Spirit it is impossible to know God or the Lord Jesus Christ. That is why you must be born again of, and be baptized with the Holy Spirit.

Cardinal reason three: to see and enter the kingdom of God

To be born again of the Holy Spirit is a mandatory requirement to enter into the kingdom of God. Matthew 6:33 and John 3:3,

5–7 declare that the process of seeking the Kingdom of God requires the believer to be born again.

Matthew 6:33: "But seek ye first the kingdom of God and His righteousness, and all these things shall be added to you."

John 3:3: "Jesus answered and said to him 'Most assuredly, I say to you, unless one is born again, he cannot see the kingdom of God.'"

John 5–7: "Jesus answered 'Most assuredly, I say to you, unless one is born of water and of the Spirit, he cannot enter the kingdom of God. That which is born of flesh is flesh, and that which is born of the Spirit is Spirit. Do not marvel that I said to you, you must be born again.'"

It is obvious that to be born again of the Holy Spirit, you must be filled and baptized with the Holy Spirit. Indeed, being filled and baptized with the Holy Spirit is the actual process of being born again of the Spirit.

Cardinal reason four: to claim the promise and receive the Gift of God.

The Holy Spirit is a major promise of God for every believer, children, the young, the old, all races and every gender of the world.

To understand this, the Old Testament book of the prophet Joel 2:28–29 has to be brought into sharp focus. "And it shall come to pass afterward that I will pour out my Spirit on all flesh; your sons and your daughters shall prophesy, your old men shall dream dreams, your young men shall see visions, and also my menservants and on my maidservants I will pour out my Spirit in those days."

In Luke 24:49, The Lord Jesus reminded the believer about this same promise of the Father, stating, "Behold, I send the promise of my Father upon you; but tarry in the city of Jerusalem until you are endued with power from on high." The author desires you to look closely and see how the Lord Jesus kept emphasizing the promise for the believers.

John 14:16–17: "And I will pray the Father, and He will give you another Helper, that He may abide with you forever, even the Spirit of truth, whom the world cannot receive, because it neither sees Him nor knows Him, but you know Him, for He dwells with you and will be in you."

John 14:26: "But the Helper, the Holy Spirit, whom the Father will send in my name, He will teach you all things, and bring to your remembrance all things that I said to you."

See the promise again in John 15:26: "But when the Helper comes, whom I shall send to you from the Father, the Spirit of truth who proceeds from the Father, He will testify of Me."

The promise is emphasized and further clarified in John 16:13–14: "However, when He, the Spirit of truth, has come, He will guide you into all truth; for He will not speak on His own authority, but whatever He hears He will speak; and He will tell you things to come. He will glorify Me, for He will take of what is Mine and declare it to you."

As the time of the fulfillment of the promise neared, the Lord Jesus expressly told the believers to prepare themselves for the promise. He revealed in Acts 1: 4–5, 8 more details about the promise.

Acts 1:4–5: "And being assembled together with them, He commanded them not to depart from Jerusalem, but to wait for the promise of the Father, 'Which,' He said, 'you have heard from me, for John truly baptized with water, but you shall be baptized with the Spirit not many days from now.'"

Acts 1:8: "But you shall receive power when the Holy Spirit has come upon you; and you shall be witnesses to me in Jerusalem, and in all Judea and Samaria, and to the end of the earth."

Finally, in Acts 2:1–4, the promise of God was faithfully and magnificently fulfilled on the believers. "Now when the day of Pentecost had fully come, they were all with one accord in one place, and suddenly there came a sound from heaven, as of a rushing mighty wind, and it filled the whole house where they were sitting. Then there appeared to them divided tongues, as of fire, and one sat upon each of them, and they were all filled with the Holy Spirit and began to speak with other tongues, as the Spirit gave them utterance."

Just as He baptized the saints (believers) of old, the Lord Jesus will baptize you with the Holy Spirit today, for Jesus Christ of yesterday is the same today and forever.

In Acts 2:38–39, apostle Peter declares, "Then Peter said to them, 'Repent, and let everyone of you be baptized in the name of Jesus Christ for the remission of sins; and you shall receive the gift of the Holy Spirit. For the promise is to you and to your children, and to all who are afar off, as many as the Lord our God will call.'"

Beloved, the Holy Spirit is God's personal special gift to you and your children. Please receive your gift and live a blessed and anointed life.

Cardinal Reason five: to be a true worshipper of God.

John 4:23–24: "The hour is coming and now is, when the true worshippers will worship the Father in Spirit and in Truth;

for the Father is seeking such to worship Him. God is Spirit and those that worship Him must worship Him in Spirit and in Truth."

Here it is evident that God Himself requires believers to worship Him in the Holy Spirit and in Truth. It is impossible to worship in the Holy Spirit if you are not baptized with the Holy Spirit. Remember that the true worshippers must worship God in the way God wants to be worshipped, and that is in Spirit and in Truth.

The good news is that it is the will of God to baptize you with His Spirit in the name of his Holy Son, Jesus Christ, to enable you to worship Him in Spirit. There is a difference between being happy and having a good time in church and worshipping God in Spirit and in Truth.

John 16:14: "He (Holy Spirit) will glorify me, for He will take of what is mine and declare it to you." Here the Lord Jesus declared that the Holy Spirit is the glorifier, therefore, Holy Spirit baptism offers the believer the opportunity to glorify God.

The author submits that to worship God in Spirit and in Truth, you must be filled and baptized with the Holy Spirit of God.

Cardinal reason six: to be anointed.

The anointing comes only by the Holy Spirit. Acts 10:38: "God anointed Jesus of Nazareth with the Holy Spirit and with power who went about doing good and healing all that were oppressed of the Devil; for God was with Him."

It is evident that God anointed the Lord Jesus Christ not with words of wisdom nor rhetoric ability but solely with the Holy Spirit. The anointing, the yolk destroying power of God,

28

the burden lifting power and devil-chasing power of the believer is received only through the Holy Spirit of God. God wants to anoint you with power but the only way you can be anointed is to be filled and baptized with the Holy Spirit. The power is yours. Get your anointing today in the name of Jesus.

Cardinal reason seven: to receive your God-given spiritual authority (exousia) and power (dunamis).

The Holy Spirit is the believer's source of spiritual authority (*exousia*). The new life in Christ is all brought about by the work and power of the Holy Spirit in the believer.

Second Corinthians 5:17: "Therefore, if anyone be in Christ, he is a new creation, old things have passed away, behold, all things have become new.

The new transformed life in the believer is brought about by the power and the working of the Holy Spirit which enables the believer to do all things including changing the old way of life to the new Christ-like way of life. The Holy Spirit brings the fruit of the Spirit to the believer.

Galatians 5:22–23: "But the fruit of the Spirit is love, joy, peace, longsuffering, kindness, goodness, faithfulness, gentleness, self-control. Against such there is no law."

As the believer practices the Fruit of the Spirit, a new and beautiful person emerges.

1 Peter 5:8 says, "Be sober, be vigilant; because your adversary the devil walks about like a roaring lion, seeking whom he may devour." The believer is constantly under attack by the prowling devourer. You need the Holy Spirit power to bind and cast out that prowling devourer.

In addition to this, the believer has to wrestle with powers and principalities, wickedness in high places as revealed in Ephesians 6:12, "For we do not wrestle against flesh and blood, but against principalities, against powers against the rulers of the darkness of this age, against spiritual hosts of wickedness in the heavenly places."

Under such constant barrage of spiritual attacks, every believer needs special spiritual power to fight and win these battles, and the only way to fight the spiritual war is to have the Holy Spirit to deal with evil spirits. You need the power of the Holy Spirit in the name of the Lord Jesus to cast these evil spirits out. You need the power of the Holy Spirit to resist the Devil himself to flee from you as James 4:7 reveals: "Therefore, submit to God. Resist the devil and he will flee from you."

You need the Holy Spirit power to give you boldness to witness and be a Christian worker. The good news is that, all the power you'll need is given to you when the Holy Spirit comes to you as revealed by the Lord in Acts 1:8: "But you shall receive power when the Holy Spirit has come upon you; and you shall be witnesses to me in Jerusalem, and in all Judea and Samaria, and to the end of the earth."

The author concludes that, to receive the power and authority of God, you must be filled and baptized with the Holy Spirit of God.

Cardinal reason eight: to pray in the Holy Spirit.

The believer must pray in the Holy Spirit. How can you pray in Spirit without the Holy Spirit? Let me clear some anomalies about praying in the Holy Spirit.

a. You can pray in unknown tongues, and that is praying in the Spirit. But, it is not the only way to pray in the Spirit. The apostle Paul declares in 1 Corinthians 14:15: "I'll pray with the Spirit, and I will also pray with the understanding. I will sing with the Spirit, and I will also sing with the understanding."

b. You can pray in the language that you understand and as long as you are filled and baptized with the Holy Spirit, the Holy Spirit intercedes and helps you to pray the effective prayer of faith.

That is also praying in the Spirit as seen above and also revealed in Romans 8:26, which says, "Likewise the Spirit also helps in our weakness. For we do not know what we should pray for as we ought, but the Spirit Himself makes intercession for us with groanings that cannot be uttered."

Another example is seen in Daniel 6:10 & 10:12.

Daniel 6:10: "Now when Daniel knew that the writing was signed, he went home. And in his upper room, with his window opened toward Jerusalem, he knelt down on his knees three times a day, and prayed and gave thanks before his God as was his custom since early days."

Daniel 10:12: "Then he said, do not fear, Daniel, for from the first day that you set your heart to understand, and to humble yourself before your God, your words were heard; and I have come because of your words."

After twenty-one days of praying, the angel of God appeared to Daniel and said, "From the very beginning of your prayers, God heard you."

Note that the Holy Bible does not reveal the prophet Daniel prayed in unknown tongues, and I believe he prayed in a known language facing Jerusalem toward Solomon's Temple and God heard his prayers and answered him.

However, the Bible reveals that Daniel had an excellent Spirit, which is another name for the Holy Spirit. Therefore, the author submits that to pray in the Holy Spirit by unknown tongues or by the believer's own native tongue, the believer must be filled with the Holy Spirit.

Cardinal reason nine: to receive the gifts of the Holy Spirit.

The gift of the Holy Spirit comes only by the Holy Spirit baptism. At various crusades and revivals that I've been honored and privileged to be the speaker, I have noticed that believers are seeking the gifts of the Holy Spirit. Evidently the Holy Spirit is the only one who gives the gifts. So to receive them you must first be baptized with the Holy Spirit. To work the works of God in the name of Jesus, the believer needs the gifts of the Holy Spirit.

The gifts of the Holy Spirit as listed in 1 Corinthians 12: 4–11 are: "Now there are diversities of gifts, but the same Spirit. There are differences of ministries, but the same Lord. And there are diversities of activities, but it is the same God who works all in all. But the manifestation of the Spirit is given to each one for the profit of all: for one is given the word of wisdom through the Spirit, to another the word of knowledge through the same Spirit to another faith by the same Spirit, to another gifts of healing by the same spirit, to another the working of miracles, to another prophecy, to another discerning of spirits, to another different kinds of tongues, to another the interpretation of tongues. But one and the same Spirit works all these things, distributing to each one individually as He wills."

The author submits that, the believer must earnestly desire the gifts. However, you must be filled and baptized first with the Holy Spirit. The Holy Spirit gives every believer one or more gifts.

Cardinal reason ten: to manifest the fruit of the Holy Spirit, the believer must first be filled with the Holy Spirit.

Galatians 5:22–23: "But the fruit of the Spirit is love, joy, peace, longsuffering, kindness, goodness, faithfulness, gentleness, self-control. Against such there is no law."

The fruit of the Holy Spirit reveal the character of a believer. However, the fruits are produced from within the believer by the Holy Spirit. It is evident therefore that the believer can only manifest the fruits first by being filled and baptized with the Holy Spirit. The Bible reveals that if believers love one another, the world will know that we are the disciples of the Lord Jesus Christ. Love is a primary fruit of the Holy Spirit.

Consider all the Christian virtues listed above, and you'll readily realize that to receive these holy virtues and to have the enabling power to practice them certainly requires the believer to be filled and baptized with the Holy Spirit.

Cardinal reason eleven: to receive and build your holy faith.

The Holy Spirit is the builder of the believer's supernatural (Spiritual) faith.

1 Corinthians. 12:9 says, "To another faith by the same Spirit, to another gifts of healing by the same Spirit."

The Holy Spirit imparts special supernatural faith as a gift to the believer.

Jude 1:20–21: "But you, beloved, building yourself up on your most holy faith praying in the Holy Spirit, keep yourselves in the love of God, looking for mercy of our Lord Jesus Christ unto eternal life." Verse twenty clearly reveals that the believer must build up his holy faith by praying in the Holy Spirit or by praying in unknown tongues. (i.e., by the intercession of the Holy Spirit; ref. Romans 8:26). But how can the believer pray in the Holy Spirit when he is not baptized with the Holy Spirit?

James 5:15: "And the prayer of faith will save the sick, and the Lord will raise him up. And if he has committed sins, he will be forgiven."

In Romans 8:26, it says, "Likewise the Spirit also helps in our weaknesses. For we do not know what we should pray for as we ought, but the Spirit Himself makes intercession for us with groanings which cannot be uttered."

The above Scriptures reveal that believers do not know how to pray to God as we ought to, but the believer receives help from the Holy Spirit to the extent that the believer's otherwise-impotent prayer becomes a fervent prayer of faith that brings miracles to increase the believer's faith.

The author concludes that to pray in the Spirit and to build on your holy faith, as well as to pray an effective prayer of faith, you must first be filled and baptized with the Holy Spirit.

Marvel not that I say to you, you must be baptized with the Holy Spirit. The promise is yours. Claim it now in the name of the Lord Jesus.

Cardinal reason twelve: to receive the eternal supernatural seal.

The Holy Spirit is God's seal on the believer.

Ephesians 1: 13–14: "In Him you also trusted, after you heard the word of truth, the gospel of your salvation; in whom also, having believed, you were sealed with the Holy Spirit of promise, who is the guarantee of inheritance until the redemption of the purchased possession, to the praise of His glory.

Here apostle Paul reveals that the believer is sealed or receives the seal of God by the Holy Spirit. This means that when the believer is filled and baptized with the Holy Spirit, you receive the seal of God whereby you become the authentic child of God through Jesus Christ.

The apostle Paul confirms this in 2 Corinthians 1:21–22. "He who establishes us with you in Christ and has anointed us is God who also has sealed us and given us the Spirit in our hearts as a deposit."

Every country or state puts its seal on its property to indicate possession and authenticity. Therefore, in a similar way, God puts his seal, which is the Holy Spirit, on every believer to indicate that you, the believer, are the authentic property of God through Jesus Christ. By this seal the believer is set apart for the praise and glory of God. This process is also referred to as sanctification.

Cardinal reason thirteen: it's a command from God

Ephesians 5:17–18: "Therefore do not be unwise, but understand what the will of the Lord is. And do not be drunk with wine, in which is dissipation; but be filled with the Spirit."

Now here is a revelation for you: to be or not to be filled with the Holy Spirit of God is not an option. God actually commands that you, the believer, must "*be filled with the spirit.*" It is one of God's many special and beautiful commands. Therefore, please obey your Father's command. In order to fulfill this command, it is obvious that you must be filled and baptized with the Holy Spirit.

Cardinal reason fourteen: to be protected from demonic attacks and demon possession

The Holy Spirit protects the believer from being demon- or Satan-possessed. Without the Holy Spirit the believer or the unbeliever is an easy and preferred target for demonic and satanic attack and possession. The Bible reveals that demons attack and possess babies, children, teenagers, young and old alike. It is therefore necessary for you to know that God desires to fill your children, teenagers, young and adults with the Holy Spirit. This is clearly revealed in Acts 2:38–39.

"Then Peter said to them, 'Repent, and let every one of you be baptized in the name of Jesus Christ for the remission of sins, and you shall receive the gift of the Holy Spirit. For the promise is to you and your children, and to all who are afar off, as many as the Lord our God will call.'"

When your children are filled with the Holy Spirit, no evil spirit can come into them. The same is true for the believer. On the contrary, let me show you what actually happens in the spirit world when one is not filled with the Holy Spirit.

Luke 11:24–26: "When an unclean spirit goes out of a man, he goes through dry places, seeking rest and finding none, he says, "I will return to my house from which I came. And when he comes, he finds it swept and put in order. Then he goes and takes with him seven other spirits more wicked than himself, and they enter and dwell there and the last state of that man is worse than the first."

What a revelation! Why should you allow eight demons to possess you and torment your life? God Himself wants to fill you with the Holy Spirit, who will prevent all demonic and satanic attacks.

Isaiah 59:19: "When the enemy comes in like a flood, the Spirit of the Lord will lift up a standard against him."

Obviously, if you don't have the Holy Spirit infilling and baptizing, no one will lift up a standard against your enemies when you come under spiritual attack. Read Isaiah 59:19 again and understand that the Holy Spirit (Spirit of the Lord) is the only one who can and will lift a standard against your adversary. Luke 3:16: "John the Baptist answered saying to them all, I indeed baptize you with water but one mightier than I is coming, whose sandals strap I am not worthy to loose. He will baptize you with the Holy Spirit and with fire."

This promise is yours and today you can be filled and baptized with the Holy Spirit of God. All you need is to first believe in the Lord Jesus Christ, that He died for you and was raised up from the dead for you. Then invite Him, and accept and receive Him as your personal Lord and Savior. Finally, earnestly ask Him to fill and baptize you with the Holy Spirit of God as He promised. Get ready, believer—you have just entered the power zone of God.

Keep praying because you are just about to be born again, filled and baptized with the Holy Spirit and with power. Don't be afraid or ashamed if the Holy Spirit makes you cry like a baby or speak in tongues or prophesy.

Cardinal reason fifteen: to be led by and walk in the Holy Spirit:

Romans 8:14 "As many as are led by the Spirit of God, these are sons of God."

Believer, you are a child of God, and you need to be led by the Spirit of your Father, which is the Holy Spirit. It is obvious that to be led by the Spirit of God you must be filled and baptized with the Holy Spirit.

Galatians 5:18: "But if you are led by the Spirit, you are not under the law."

To be led by the Spirit of God is to walk in grace and not by the law.

Galatians 5:16: "I say then, 'Walk in the Spirit and you shall not fulfill the lust of the flesh.'"

Galatians 5:25: "If we live in the Spirit, let us also walk in the Spirit."

The author declares from the above Scriptures that, to be led by and walk in the Spirit, you must be filled and baptized with the Holy Spirit. Believer, it is evident that God has very powerful reasons to fill and baptize you with the Holy Spirit as revealed in the above fifteen cardinal reasons. As you continue to study, I pray that the Holy Spirit of God may reveal more reasons to you.

Your hands have made me and fashioned me. Give me understanding, that I may learn Your commandments.
—Psalm 119:73

CHAPTER 5

Me, the Temple of God

Something caught my attention in John 1:38. John the Baptist
had disciples. One day he was with two of them when they saw
the Lord Jesus. John the Baptist spoke by the Holy Spirit, saying,
"Behold the Lamb of God."

John 1:36: At his confession of the Lord Jesus as the Lamb of
God who really takes away the sin of the world [John 1:29], the
two disciples of John the Baptist moved on to follow the Lord
Jesus." And as they beheld the Lord Jesus, it is very interesting that
the first question was, Rabbi, where do you live?

John 1:38: "Then Jesus turned, and seeing them following,
said to them, 'What do you seek?' They said, 'Rabbi' (which is to
say, when translated, Teacher), 'where are You staying?'"

God has sent His Spirit to come to the earth as the Lord Jesus
promised that the Holy Spirit should be with the believer forever.

The question therefore is this: "Where does the Holy Spirit
live here on earth?"

I strongly believe if you knew where the mighty Holy Spirit
of God lives, when He comes to you, you will generously prepare
a fine place for Him to stay.

In 2 Kings 4:8–17 it is revealed how the Shunamite woman prepared a beautiful place for God's prophet Elisha to live. She received a miracle for her goodwill toward the prophet of God.

> Now it happened one day that Elisha went to Shunem, Where there was a notable woman, and she constrained him to eat some food. So it was, as often as he passed by, that he turned in there to eat some food. And she said to her husband, "Look now, I know that this is a holy man of God, who passes by us regularly. Please, let us make a small upper room on the wall; and let us put a bed for him there, and a table and a chair and a lamp stand; so it will be, whenever he comes to us, he can turn in there." And it happened one day that he came there, and he turned in to the upper room, and lay down there. Then he said to Gehazi his servant, "Call this Shunammite woman." When he had called her, she stood before him. And he said to him, "Say now to her, Look, you have been concerned for us with all this care. What can I do for you? Do you want me to speak on your behalf to the king or to the commander of the army?" And she answered, "I dwell among my own people." So he said, "What then is to be done for her?" And Gehazi answered, "Actually, she has no son and her husband is old." And he said, "Call her." When he had called her, she stood in the doorway. Then he said, "About this time next year you shall embrace a son." And she said, "No, my lord. Man of God, do not lie to your

maidservant!" And the woman conceived and bore a son when the appointed time had come, of which Elisha had told her."

Luke 10:38–39 also reveals that Mary and her sister Martha and their brother Lazarus prepared a place for the Lord Jesus to stay anytime the Lord was in their hometown Bethany. They also received a miracle for their goodwill as revealed in Luke 10:38: "Now it happened as they went that He entered a certain village; and a certain woman named Martha welcomed Him into her home. And she had a sister called Mary, who also sat at Jesus feet and heard His word."

The resurrection of Lazarus is one of the mighty miracles Mary and Martha received for their good works toward the Lord Jesus.

John 11:1, 5, 14, 43–44

John 11:1: "Now a certain man was sick, Lazarus of Bethany, the town of Mary and her sister Martha."

John 11:5: "Now Jesus loved Martha and her sister and Lazarus."

John 11:14: "Then Jesus said to them plainly, 'Lazarus is dead.'"

John 11:43–44: "Now when He had said these things, He cried with a loud voice, 'Lazarus come forth.' And he who had died came out bound hand and foot with grave clothes, and his face was wrapped with a cloth. Jesus said to them, 'Loose him, and let him go.'"

I believe that if you prepare a place for the Spirit of God to live, you will receive miracles and indeed, you will live a rhythm of daily miracles, for greater is He that is truly in you than he that is in the world.

Marvel not when I say to you that many believers and unbelievers are not sure where the Holy Spirit lives. Hence, they don't prepare a place for Him nor do they expect His arrival.

Consequently they do not also know how to treat Him with reverence that He deserves but like every poor host or hostess, some grieve Him, some quench Him and some don't even open the door for Him to enter and keep Him standing outside knocking at the door. Some even blaspheme against Him and commit the unpardonable sin.

Matthew 12:32: "Anyone who speaks a word against the Son of Man will be forgiven, but whoever speaks against the Holy Spirit will not be forgiven, either in this age or in the age to come."

The more you know about the Holy Spirit, the more you surrender to Him. Only He can and will put your life back together, back on track, and fix your problems, and He will bind broken hearts, homes, lives, hopes, expectations, and dreams in the name of the Lord Jesus to the glory of God.

Where Does the Holy Spirit of God Live?

The Holy Spirit lives in the believer's body. Before I make it even more specific, let me share with you some Scriptures to illuminate and animate the searching mind.

Nehemiah 9:30: "Yet for many years You had patience with them, and testified against them by Your Spirit in Your prophets. Yet they would not listen. Therefore you gave them into the hand of the people of the lands."

Isaiah 63:11: "Then he remembered the days of old, Moses and his people, saying, 'Where is He who brought them up out of the sea with the shepherd of His flock. Where is He who put

His Holy Spirit within them?'" It is evident that the Holy Spirit indwelt the Old Testament prophets.

John 14:17 reveals that "The Spirit of Truth, whom the world cannot receive, because it neither sees Him nor knows Him; but you know Him, for He dwells with you and will be in you." In this Scripture, the Lord Jesus states that the Holy Spirit *will be in you*. Concerning various theological ("theo-logic") doctrines of "upon," "on," "within" and "around," the author submits that the Holy Spirit always in-dwells the believer, from Genesis to Revelation. The Bible reveals King Saul to be the only person from whom the Holy Spirit departed.

Acts 2:4 states, "And they were all filled with the Holy Spirit and began to speak with other tongues, as the Spirit gave them utterance." The act of filling has the connotation of something empty on the inside being filled with something from the outside. Here, the Holy Spirit from God is filling the disciples in the upper room.

Romans 8:11: "But if the Spirit of Him who raised Jesus from the dead dwells in you, He who raised Christ from the dead will also give life to your mortal bodies through His Spirit who dwells in you."

1 Corinthians 3:16–17: "Do you not know that you are the temple of God and that the Spirit of God dwells in you? If anyone defiles the temple of God, God will destroy him. For the temple of God is holy, which temple you are."

1 Corinthians 6:19: "Or do you not know that your body is the temple of the Holy Spirit who is in you, whom you have from God, and you are not your own?"

Again the apostle Paul reveals that the Spirit of God dwells in you and emphatically declares that your body is the temple in which the Holy Spirit of God lives. Therefore, keep your body holy and healthy for divine habitation and be blessed forever as God's sanctified vessel of honor for His use and glory.

Specific Habitation

Let us imagine you are driving a beautiful car. You have total control and are happily cruising on the highway. But first, to drive this car, you have to be in the car, of course.

In a similar way you are the car, and the Holy Spirit is in you, driving you along route 66 (like the sixty-six books of the Bible). You are not just anywhere in the car, driving. There is a specific place allocated for the driver, which is referred to as the driver's seat, from which you direct the entire vehicle.

In a similar way, the Bible reveals the exact part of the body where the Holy Spirit lives from where he directs, guides, instructs, comforts, and protects the believer to accomplish successfully, the will of God in your life. That part is the *heart,* as stated in Galatians 4:6: "And because you are sons, God has sent forth the Spirit of His Son into your hearts, crying out, Abba, Father!" Second Corinthians 1:22 reiterates that the Holy Spirit resides in the heart of the believer as a deposit. "Who also has sealed us and given us the Spirit in our hearts as a deposit."

Based on the Scriptures above, we see that the Holy Spirit lives inside the believer's body. He doesn't just hover above the head of the believer, nor is He floating in the air around the believer. He comes to the believer from God and dwells inside the heart of the believer to guide, teach, and keep the believer in your walk with the Lord Jesus Christ.

Now it becomes much clearer to understand the promise of God when He said, "I'll never leave you nor forsake you." and again He promised, "The Lord shall be with you when you go out and when you come in." (Deuteronomy 31:8)

It becomes even more exciting when you realize and understand the promise of the Lord Jesus in Matthew 28:20: "Lo, I am with you always." All these promises are based on the truth that the Holy Spirit, who is God, dwells in your heart, and everywhere you go He is with you. Praise God—you can't leave home without Him.

CHAPTER 6

Holy Names of the Holy Spirit

Deuteronomy. 29:29 reveals, "The secret things belong to the Lord our God, but those things which are revealed belong to us and to our children forever, that we may do all the words of this law."

Whereas we are, in this present dispensation, not under the law but in grace, God is still the same and is revealing more of Himself or the "secret things of the Lord our God" to us.

The apostle Paul reveals more of this truth in 1 Corinthians 2:10–12: "But God has revealed them to us through His Spirit. For the Spirit searches all things, yes, the deep things of God. For what man knows the things of a man except the spirit of the man which is in him? Even so no one knows the things of God except the Spirit of God. Now we have received, not the spirit of the world, but the Spirit who is from God, that we might know the things that have been freely given to us by God."

The above, simply translated, means the Holy Spirit reveals the inner thoughts and heart of God to the believer. Therefore the things that the Holy Spirit does, are things that God is doing in the name of the Lord Jesus Christ. Remember, the revealed things belong to us. The Jehovistic names of Jehovah God, relate to what He does. For example, when God heals, we call Him Jehovah Rapha. That is, God, the healer. When He supplies needs, we call

Him, Jehovah Jireh and because He is the source of peace, we call Him Jehovah Shalom.

In a very similar way, the Holy Spirit has other names that relate to what He is doing or what He does. Remember that the Holy Spirit is the Spirit of God.

Now, before we get into the Holy names of the Holy Spirit, the author wishes to explain one important truth.

In John 4:24 we learn that God is Spirit. But we also know that Satan, the Devil himself, is Spirit. In the book of Leviticus 11:44–45 and 1 Peter 1:15–16, we learn that the Lord our God is Holy.

Leviticus 11:44–45: "For I am the Lord your God. You shall therefore sanctify yourselves, and you shall be holy; for I am holy. Neither shall you defile yourselves with any creeping thing that creeps on the earth. For I am the Lord who brings you up out of the Land of Egypt, to be your God. You shall therefore be holy, for I am holy."

1 Peter 1:15–16: "But as He who called you is holy, you also be holy in all your conduct, because it is written, be holy, for I am holy."

Therefore, the author declares the following:

- God is Spirit.
- God is Holy.
- Therefore, God is Holy Spirit.

For your knowledge, please note also that

- Satan, the Devil, is spirit.
- Satan, the Devil, is evil.
- Therefore, Satan, the Devil, is an evil spirit.

Let us now look at the names of the Holy Spirit. The author reminds you that these may not be the entire exhaustive list of names of the Holy Spirit. Therefore, should you identify more names of the Holy Spirit in the Holy Bible, please add to the list in your copy of this book. These names are sometimes also referred to as titles of the Holy Spirit.

For clarity, easy assimilation, and understanding, the author has grouped these names into two categories, the Old Testament and New Testament of the Holy Spirit.

Old Testament names of the Holy Spirit

Spirit of God. This is revealed as the Spirit hovering above the waters in the creative moments by God in Genesis 1:2: "The earth was without form and void and darkness was on the face of the deep And the Spirit of God was hovering over the face of the waters."

Also seen in Genesis 41:38: And Pharaoh said to his servants, 'Can we find such a one as this, a man in whom is the Spirit of God?'"

Breath of Life, found in the creation of Adam in Genesis 2:7: "And the Lord God formed man of the dust of the ground, and breathed into his nostrils the breath of life; and man became a living being."

My Spirit, also revealed in Genesis 6:3 and Isaiah 44:3. Genesis 6:3: "And the Lord said, 'My Spirit shall not strive with man forever, for he is indeed flesh; yet his days shall be one hundred and twenty years.'" Isaiah 44:3: "For I will pour water on him who is thirsty, and floods on the dry ground I will pour my Spirit on your descendants, and my blessing on the offspring."

Spirit of the Lord. First Samuel 16:13 reveals this truth: "Then Samuel took the horn of oil and anointed him in the midst of his brothers; and the Spirit of the Lord came upon David from that day forward. So Samuel arose and went to Ramah." Also in Micah 2:7: "You are named the house of Jacob: 'Is the Spirit of the Lord restricted? Are these His doing? Do not my words do good to him who walks uprightly?'"

Your Good Spirit, seen in Nehemiah 9:20: "You also gave Your good Spirit to instruct them, and did not withhold Your manna from their mouth, and gave them water for their thirst."

Your Spirit, revealed in Nehemiah 9:30: "Yet for many years You had patience with them, and testified against them by Your Spirit in Your prophets. Yet they would not listen; therefore You gave them into the hand of the peoples of the lands."

Breath of The Almighty: Job 32:8 "But there is a spirit in man, and the breath of the Almighty gives him understanding." Job 33:4 "The Spirit of God has made me, and the breath of the Almighty gives me life."

Holy Spirit. In Psalm 51:11, King David reveals that the Spirit of the Lord is the Holy Spirit. "Do not cast me away from Your presence, and do not take Your Holy Spirit from me."

Generous Spirit. Psalm 51:12 says, "Restore to me the joy of Your salvation, and uphold me with Your generous Spirit."

Spirit of Creation. This is evident in Psalm 104:30: "You send forth Your Spirit, they are created; And You renew the face of the earth." This is a powerful revelation that the Holy Spirit of God is a creator.

Lamp of the Lord, seen in Proverbs 20:27: "The spirit of a man is the lamp of the Lord, Searching all the inner depths of his heart." This is more than conscience, as proposed by others. This is the Holy Spirit of God, who searches even the fallible conscience of the human being.

The Holy *Spirit* is the reader of the intent of the heart and mind of human beings. Bear in mind that the unregenerate person does not comprehend the things of God, indeed it is foolishness to such a person. The Bible reveals that such a man without the Holy Spirit to regenerate the heart indeed has a natural heart, which is desperately wicked and stony.

Spirit of Judgment and Burning, revealed in Isaiah 4:4: "When the Lord has washed away the filth of the daughters of Zion, and purged the blood of Jerusalem from her midst, by the spirit of judgment and by the spirit of burning."

Spirit of Wisdom and Understanding. Isaiah 11:2 reveals this truth. "The Spirit of the Lord shall rest upon him, the Spirit of wisdom and understanding, the Spirit of counsel and might, the Spirit of knowledge and of the fear of the Lord."

Spirit of Counsel and Might. Again Isaiah 11:2 reveals this truth and confirmed by the Lord Jesus in Acts 1:8: "But you shall receive power when the Holy Spirit has come upon you."

Spirit of Knowledge and of Fear of the Lord, continued in Isaiah 11:2 (see Spirit of Wisdom and Understanding above).

Spirit of Justice in Isaiah 28:6: "For a spirit of justice to him who sits in judgment, And for strength to those who turn back to battle at the gate."

Spirit from on High, revealed in Isaiah 32:15 and confirmed by the Lord Jesus in Luke 24:49. Isaiah 32:15: "Until the Spirit is poured upon us from on high, and the wilderness becomes a fruitful field." Luke 24:49: "Behold, I send the promise of my Father upon you; but tarry in the city of Jerusalem until you are endued with power from on high."

His Spirit, as seem in Isaiah 48:16: "Come near to me, hear this: I have not spoken in secret from the beginning; from the time that it was, I was there. And now the Lord God and His Spirit have sent me."

Spirit of the Lord God. This is evident in Isaiah 61:1: "The Spirit of the Lord God is upon me, because the Lord has anointed me to preach good tidings to the poor; He has sent me to heal the brokenhearted, to proclaim liberty to the captives, and the opening of the prison to those who are bound."

His Holy Spirit, grieved by the rebellious in Isaiah 63:10–11: "But they rebelled and grieved His Holy Spirit; so He turned Himself against them as an enemy, and He fought against them. Then He remembered the days of old, Moses and his people saying: 'Where is He who brought them up out of the sea with the shepherd of His flock? Where is He who put His Holy Spirit within them?'"

A New Spirit, revealed in Ezekiel 11:19: "Then I will give them one heart, and I will put a new spirit within them, and take the stony heart out of their flesh, and give them a heart of flesh."

Spirit of the Holy God. This is revealed by the queen of King Belteshazzar in Daniel 5:11: "There is a man in your kingdom in whom is the Spirit of the Holy God."

Excellent Spirit. In Daniel 5:12, "Inasmuch as an excellent spirit, knowledge, understanding, interpreting dreams, solving riddles, and explaining enigmas were found in this Daniel, whom the king named Belteshazzar, now let Daniel be called, and he will give the interpretation."

The same queen was used to reveal that the Spirit of our God is an excellent Spirit and goes on to list some of the gifts of the Holy Spirit that were given to the prophet Daniel. These spiritual gifts include knowledge, interpretation of dreams, solving riddles, and explaining enigmas.

Spirit of Grace. In Zechariah 12:10, the prophet prophesied concerning when the Holy Spirit will be poured out on the House of David and on the inhabitants of Jerusalem and revealed that period will be the dispensation of grace and accordingly called the Holy Spirit, the Spirit of grace.

Living water. A powerful revelation in Zechariah 14:8 and confirmed by the Lord Jesus in John 4:10, as well as John 7:38.

John 4:10: "Jesus answered and said to her, 'If you knew the gift of God, and who it is who says to you, "Give me a drink," you would have asked Him, and He would have given you living water.'" John 7:38: "He who believes in me, as the Scriptures has said, out of his heart will flow rivers of living water."

New Testament Names of the Holy Spirit

Spirit of God, revealed at the baptism of the Lord Jesus in Matthew 3:16: "Then Jesus, when He had been baptized, came up immediately from the water; and behold, the heavens were opened to Him, and He saw the Spirit of God descending like a dove and alighting upon Him."

Dove, also revealed beautifully in Matthew 3:16 (see Spirit of God above).

Spirit of Your Father. The Lord Jesus revealed this while preparing the disciples for work in Matthew 10:20: "For it is not you who speak, but the Spirit of your Father who speaks in you."

The Spirit. This was revealed by the Lord Jesus when He prescribed the terrible eternal consequences of blasphemy of the Holy Spirit of God in Matthew 12:31: "Therefore I say to you, every sin and blasphemy will be forgiven men, but the blasphemy against the Spirit will not be forgiven men."

The Holy Spirit. The angel Gabriel revealed this to Mary during the enunciation. Luke 1:35: "And the angel answered and said to her, 'The Holy Spirit will come upon you, and the power of the Highest will overshadow you; therefore, also, that Holy one who is to be born will be called the Son of God.'"

Power of the Lord, in Luke 5:17: "Now it happened on a certain day as He was teaching, that there were Pharisees and teachers of the law sitting by, who had come out of every town of Galilee, Judea, and Jerusalem. And the power of the Lord was present to heal them."

The Finger of God, revealed in Luke 11:20: "But if I cast out demons with the finger of God, surely the kingdom of God has come upon you."

Rivers of Living Water. John 7:38 reveals this truth: "He who believes in me, as the Scripture has said out of his heart will flow rivers of living water."

The Helper, as seen in John 14:26: "But the Helper, the Holy Spirit, whom the Father will send in my name, He will teach you all things, and bring to your remembrance all things that I said to you."

Spirit of Truth, in John 14:17: "Even the Spirit of truth, whom the world cannot receive, because it neither sees Him nor knows Him; but you know Him, for He dwells with you and will be in you." Here the Lord Jesus reveals the Holy Spirit as the spirit of Truth. Compare the spirit of lies which is the sure spirit of Lucifer, also known as Satan (see John 8:44).

Tongues of Fire, revealed on the day of Pentecost in the upper-room Holy Spirit baptism experience. Acts 2:3: "Then there appeared to them divided tongues as of fire and one sat upon each of them."

Promised Holy Spirit. This is revealed in Acts 2:33 and in Galatians 3:14. Acts 2:33: "Therefore being exalted to the right hand of God, and having received from the Father the promise of the Holy Spirit, He poured out this which you now see and hear." Galatians 3:14: "That the blessing of Abraham might come upon the Gentiles in Christ Jesus, that we might receive the promise of the Spirit through faith."

The Gift. Apostle Peter refers to the Holy Spirit as the Gift in Acts 2:38: "Then Peter said to them, 'Repent, and let everyone of you be baptized in the name of Jesus Christ for the remission of sins; and you shall receive the gift of the Holy Spirit.'"

God. In the ultimate revelation of the Holy Spirit in Acts 5:4, apostle Peter declares that the Holy Spirit is God. "While it remained, was it not your own? And after it was sold, was it not in your own control? Why have you conceived this thing in your heart? You have not lied to men but to God."

This is why it is an abomination to lie to a Holy Spirit-filled anointed believer. The Devil deceives you to think he or she is an ordinary person and leads you to sin and curse and to catastrophic consequences. Can you imagine the amount of blessings believers have missed from God because believers lie so much to one another?

Spirit of Holiness. The apostle Paul reveals that the Holy Spirit is the spirit of Holiness in Romans 1:4: "And declared to be the

Son of God with power, according to the Spirit of holiness, by the resurrection from the dead."

Spirit of Life. Romans 8:2: "For the law of the Spirit of life in Christ Jesus has made me free from the law of sin and death." Here the Holy Spirit is revealed as the Spirit of life in the Lord Jesus Christ. Any believer who receives the Holy Spirit receives the Spirit of Life.

Spirit of Christ. Romans 8:9: "But you are not in the flesh but in the Spirit, if indeed the Spirit of God dwells in you. Now if anyone does not have the Spirit of Christ, he is not His."

His Spirit Who Lives in You. Romans 8:11 reveals this powerful revelation of the Holy Spirit of God that lives in you. (See also 1 Corinthians 6:19.) Romans 8:11: "But if the Spirit of Him who raised Jesus from the dead dwells in you, He who raised Christ from the dead will also give life to your mortal bodies through His Spirit who dwells in you."

Spirit of Adoption. Romans 8:15: "For you did not receive the spirit of bondage again to fear, but you received the Spirit of adoption by whom we cry out, Abba, Father." Here the Holy Spirit is the one that effects the believer's adoption process into the family of God.

The Spirit Himself. Romans 8:26 reveals this truth: "Likewise the Spirit also helps in our weaknesses. For we do not know what we should pray for as we ought, but the Spirit Himself makes intercession for us with groanings which cannot be uttered."

The Spirit who is from God. First Corinthians 2:12: "Now we have received, not the spirit of the world, but the Spirit who is from God, that we might know the things that have been freely given to us by God."

Spirit of our God. Seen in 1 Corinthians 6:11, which reads, "And such were some of you. But you were washed, but you were sanctified, but you were justified in the name of the Lord Jesus and by the Spirit of our God."

One Spirit. As in 1 Corinthians 12:13: "For by one Spirit we were all baptized into one body—whether Jews or Greeks, whether slaves or free—and have all been made to drink into one Spirit."

Deposit, as revealed in 2 Corinthians 1:22: "Who also has sealed us and given us the Spirit in our hearts as a deposit."

Spirit of the Living God. Revealed in 2 Corinthians 3:3: "Clearly you are manifestly an epistle of Christ, ministered by us, written not with ink but by the Spirit of the living God, not on tablets of stone but on tablets of flesh, that is of the heart."

Spirit of the Lord. We read this in 2 Corinthians 3:18: "But we all, with unveiled face, beholding as in a mirror the glory of the Lord, are being transformed into the same image from glory to glory, just as by the Spirit of the Lord."

Spirit of His Son, revealed in Galatians 4:6: "And because you are sons, God has sent forth the Spirit of His Son into your hearts, crying out, 'Abba, Father!'"

Holy Spirit of Promise. Ephesians 1:13: "In Him you also trusted, after you heard the word of truth, the gospel of your salvation; in whom also, having believed, you were sealed with the Holy Spirit of promise."

Spirit of Wisdom and Revelation. Ephesians 1:17: "That the God of our Lord Jesus Christ the Father of glory, may give to you the spirit of wisdom and revelation in the knowledge of Him."

Holy Spirit of God. In Ephesians 4:30: "You are commanded not to grieve the Holy Spirit of God. And do not grieve the Holy Spirit of God, by whom you were sealed for the day of redemption."

Spirit of Jesus Christ. Powerfully revealed in Philippians 1:19: "For I know that this will turn out for my salvation through your prayer and the supply of the Spirit of Jesus Christ."

Spirit of Love, Power, and Sound Mind. Second Timothy 1:7: "For God has not given us a spirit of fear, but of power and of love and of a sound mind."

Eternal Spirit. Hebrew 9:14: "How much more shall the blood of Christ, who through the eternal Spirit offered Himself without spot to God, purge your conscience from dead works to serve the living God?"

Spirit of Grace. Hebrew 10:29: "Of how much worse punishment, do you suppose, will he be thought worthy who has trampled the Son of God underfoot, counted the blood of the covenant by which he was sanctified a common thing, and insulted the Spirit of grace?"

Holy Spirit. First Peter 1:12 reveals this: "To them it was revealed that, not to themselves, but to us they were ministering the things which now have been reported to you through those who have preached the gospel to you by the Holy Spirit sent from heaven-things which angels desire to look into."

Spirit of Glory. First Peter 4:14: "If you are reproached for the name of Christ, blessed are you for the Spirit of glory and of God rests upon you. On their part He is blasphemed, but on your part He is glorified."

The Anointing. First John 2:27 reveals this truth, sometimes also called the unction. "But the anointing which you have received from Him abides in you, and you do not need that anyone teach you; but as the same anointing teaches you concerning all things, and is true, and is not a lie, and just as it has taught you, you will abide in Him."

Having revealed these other names of the *Holy* Spirit, it is my hope that as you study the Word of God, the activities of the Holy Spirit will become clearer and more evident to augment your understanding of the Holy Scriptures. It will also increase your anointing.

Cast your burden on the LORD, and He shall sustain you; He shall never permit the righteous to be moved.
—Psalm 55:22

CHAPTER 7

Symbols (Emblems) of the Holy Spirit

The word *emblem* means "object or representation that stands for or suggests something else."

The word *symbol* means "something that stands for or suggests something else by reason of relationship, association, convention, or resemblance especially a visible sign of something invisible."

Symbols or emblems are used to represent the Holy Spirit throughout the Holy Bible. The believer needs to know and understand these symbols to rightly divide (interpret) the word of God. In this chapter, the author will share with you many of the powerful symbols in the Holy Scriptures used to represent the Holy Spirit of God.

Fire

Fire is symbolic of the Holy Spirit as revealed in the following scriptures: Luke 3:16: "John answered, saying to all, 'I indeed baptize with water, but one mightier than I is coming whose sandal strap I am not worthy to loose, He will baptize you with the Holy Spirit and with *fire*" (emphasis added). Here the symbol or emblem being used to symbolize the Holy Spirit is *fire*.

In Exodus 3:2, God uses fire as a symbol of the Holy Spirit: "And the angel of the Lord appeared to him in a flame of fire from the midst of a bush. So he looked, and behold, the bush burned with fire but the bush was not consumed."

Fire: the Burning Bush

The Lord appeared to Moses in the *burning bush,* but the bush was not consumed. In like manner, the Holy Spirit is like fire in the believer, and the believer is hot for Jesus, as in the proverbial saying, "On fire for Jesus." Many more Christians ought to be on fire for Jesus. When you are on fire for Jesus, you are doing the work of God in the Spirit, such as testifying of Him to the unsaved person, ministering to one another, and supporting the ministry. The believer is on fire for Jesus but is not consumed.

Again we read in Acts 2:2–4: "And suddenly there came a sound from Heaven, as of a rushing mighty wind, and it filled the whole house where they were sitting. Then there appeared to them divided tongues of fire, and one sat upon each of them. And they were all filled with the Holy Spirit and began to speak with other tongues as the spirit gave them utterance."

Here tongues of fire are symbolic of the overflow of the Holy Spirit infilling leading to, as it were, the baptism in the Holy Spirit. Which is to say the believers were fully filled and immersed in the Holy Spirit anointing.

Dove

Another symbol or emblem of the Holy Spirit is the dove.

Numerous examples of this exist in the Bible. Matthew 3:16 states, "When He had been baptized, Jesus came up immediately from the water; behold the heavens were opened to Him and he saw the Spirit of God descending like a dove and alighting upon Him." John 1:32, John bore witness, saying, "I saw the Spirit descending from heaven like a dove, and He remained upon Him."

The *dove* is used as the universal symbol of peace.

Here the Holy Spirit is symbolized by a dove returning to Noah's ark with the olive leaf in its mouth, signifying that all is well on earth. Genesis 8:10–11: "And he waited yet another seven days, and again he sent the dove out from the ark. Then the dove came to him in the evening, and behold, a freshly plucked olive leaf was in her mouth; and Noah knew that the waters had abated from the earth."

Anointing Oil

Elaion is a Greek word that specifically refers to olive oil. Specially consecrated olive oil, hereafter referred to as anointing oil, for various spiritual uses, is prevalent in the Old and New Testaments. The Anointing Oil is another emblem of the Holy Spirit.

Examples of this abound in the Holy Scripture: James 5:14–15 states, "Is anyone among you sick? Let him call for the elders of the church and let them pray over him anointing him with oil in the name of the Lord and the prayer of faith will save the sick and the Lord will raise him up, and if he has committed sins, he will be forgiven."

Mark 6:13 states "And they cast out many demons, and anointed with oil many who were sick and healed them."

We are told in Matthew 6:17, "But you, when you fast, anoint your head and wash your face," and here we see the Lord giving the believers instruction on how we should use the anointing oil when we fast.

Throughout the Bible the anointing oil has played a very important role in the believers walk with God. The prophet Samuel anointed King Saul with anointing oil and the Holy Spirit came upon King Saul.

First Samuel 10:1: "Then Samuel took a flask of oil and poured it on his head, and kissed him and said: 'Is it not because the Lord has anointed you commander over His inheritance?'"

First Samuel 10:6: "Then the spirit of the Lord will come upon you, and you will prophesy with them and be turned into another man."

First Samuel 10:10: "When they came there to the hill, there was a group of prophets to meet him; then the Spirit of God came upon him, and he prophesied among them."

Again we see clearly that the anointing oil is an authentic emblem of the Holy Spirit for ordination, consecration, dedication, and for sanctification especially for the prophets, priests, and kings to their offices. Please read Exodus 30:22–33 for more knowledge and understanding of the anointing oil.

Water

Water is also symbolic of the Holy Spirit. John 7:38–39: "He who believes in me, as the scripture has said out of his heart will flow rivers of living water. But this He spoke concerning the Spirit, whom those believing in Him would receive for the Holy Spirit was not yet given, because Jesus was not yet glorified."

The above is self-explanatory in that the Lord Jesus Christ symbolically represented the Holy Spirit with water, which shall be in the believer with the subsequent anointing which shall be released by the believer.

Again, we see in John 4:13–14 that the Lord Jesus Christ symbolized the Holy Spirit with water. In the discourse at the well, the Lord Jesus Christ witnessed to a woman saying, "Whoever drinks of this water will thirst again, but whoever drinks of the water that I shall give him will never thirst. But the water that I shall give him will become in him a fountain of water springing up into everlasting life."

Seven major observations about water symbolically reveal spiritual activities of the Holy Spirit in the dynamic transformation of the believer.

1. **Water cleanses**, as revealed in Ephesians 5:26-27: "He might sanctify and cleanse it with the washing of water by the word, that He might present it to Himself a glorious church not having spot or wrinkle or any such thing but that it should be holy and without blemish."

2. **Water washes away dirt** or defilement as revealed in Exodus 30:18–19, which says, "You shall also make a laver of bronze with its base also of bronze, for washing. You shall put it between the tabernacle of meeting and the alter. And you shall put water in it, for Aaron and his sons shall wash their hands and their feet in water from it."

3. **Water satisfies the thirsty one** as symbolized in Isaiah 44:3, "I will pour water upon him who is thirsty and

floods upon the ground. I will pour my spirit upon your offspring and my blessing upon your descendants." The invitation is given to you in Isaiah 55:1: "Ho! Everyone who thirsts, come to the waters."

4. **Water purifies** just like the universal gospel purifies. Revealed in Numbers 31:23–24: "Everything that can endure fire, you shall put through the fire and it shall be clean; and it shall be purified with the water of purification. But all that cannot endure fire you shall put through water. And you shall wash your clothes on the seventh day and be clean, and afterward you may come into the camp."

5. **Water makes living things and beings fruitful**. Here the Holy Spirit is symbolized by water as revealed by the prophet Ezekiel (Ezekiel 47:1–12).

6. **Water maintains life**. In John 4:10–15, in the discourse with the woman at the well, the Lord Jesus Christ reveals that the water He gives symbolizing the Holy Spirit will be a source of everlasting life. It is also seen that the word of God cleanses and maintains life, for the word is spirit as seen in John 6:63: "It is the Spirit who gives life; the flesh profits nothing. The word that I speak to you are spirit, and they are life." The author concludes that water, which is symbolic of the Holy Spirit, is also symbolic of the word of God, which maintains life in the believer.

Water refreshes, just as the Holy Spirit refreshes. The word of God refreshes. In the book of Revelation it is revealed that the Lord Jesus Christ has a hidden name, which is "The word of God." Again, the author concludes that Jesus Christ, who is the word of God, refreshes the believer, all because if anyone is in Christ he is a new creation and all things become new. Finally, just as natural life is maintained with water (without water every living thing dies), spiritual life is also maintained with the Holy Spirit (it is the Holy Spirit who gives life as seen in John 6:63) and without the Holy Spirit a person is referred to as spiritually dead. What water is to living things, so is the Holy Spirit to a believer.

Seal

"Seal" (noun) is "a device, an attachment, or a mark used to confirm, validate or authenticate," according to Webster's dictionary. Seal (verb) is defined as "to attach or mark with a seal; to confirm, validity, authenticity and to make certain."

Every country, state, nation, city, or company has a seal to authenticate documents or property. The above is an example of the seal of the United States of America.

The Holy Spirit is symbolically God's seal on his property, the believer. Ephesians 1:13–14 states, "In Him you also trusted, after you heard the word of truth, the gospel of your salvation; in whom also, having believed, you were sealed with the Holy

Spirit of promise. Who is the guarantee of our inheritance until the redemption of the purchased possession, to the praise of His glory."

Second Corinthians 1:21–22 states, "Now He who establishes us with you in Christ and has anointed us is God, who also has sealed us and given us the Spirit in our heart as a deposit." Holy Spirit baptism is the confirmation, validation, and authentication of the believer that you are a true child of God in the name of Jesus.

Still, Small Voice

In 1 Kings 19:12–13, a still, small voice is used to symbolize the Holy Spirit. "And after the earthquake a fire, but the Lord was not in the fire; and after the fire a still, small voice. So it was, when Elijah heard it, that he wrapped his face in his mantle and went out and stood in the entrance of the cave. And suddenly a voice came to him, and said, 'What are you doing here, Elijah?'"

The Holy Spirit here is recognized as the voice of God within the believer for the purposes of revealing the will of God to the soul of the believer. That means the Holy Spirit is on the inside speaking, guiding, counseling, and strengthening the soul of the believer. The Holy Spirit is the voice of God within the believer and He reveals Jesus Christ and the will of God to the believer.

Finger of God

In Matthew 12:28, the Lord Jesus Christ reveals, "I cast out demons by the Spirit of God." This is beautifully symbolized in Luke 11:20, which reveals, "I cast out demons with the finger of God"

Here the finger of God is revealed as the Holy Spirit power of God that cast out demons to set believers free of oppressive, suppressive, and depressing spirits.

In Daniel 5:5-6 we read, "In the same hour the finger of a man's hand appeared and wrote opposite the lamp-stand on the plaster of the wall of the king's palace; and the king saw the part of the hand that wrote. Then the king's countenance changed, and his thoughts troubled him, so that joints of his hips were loosened and his knees knocked against each other."

John 16:8 says, "The Lord Jesus Christ speaking of the coming of the Holy Spirit said, "When He [the Holy Spirit] comes; He will convict the world of guilt in regard to sin and righteousness and judgment" (New International Version).

It is evident by the above Scriptures that the Holy Spirit is the finger of God that points or reveals the error of the sinner or finger of judgment with the ultimate intent to convict and convert the sinner. The same finger draws the sinner to the realm of repentance and to accept Jesus Christ as Lord and Savior.

The Wind

In Acts 2: 1-2, we read, "Now the day of Pentecost had fully come, they were all with one accord in one place. And suddenly there came a sound from heaven, as of a rushing, mighty wind, and it filled the whole house where they were sitting."

On the day of Pentecost, the coming of the Holy Spirit is powerfully symbolized with "*a rushing, mighty wind.*" Soon after that, they who were in the upper-room were filled with the rushing mighty Holy Spirit of God from heaven.

These are but a few powerful emblems or symbols of the Holy Spirit of God. Throughout the Holy Bible, references are made to other emblems. As you continue your studies and your walk with the Lord, you will become more familiar with the other emblems. May the Lord continue to increase your knowledge.

You shall love the LORD your God with all your heart, with all your soul, with all your strength, and with all your mind, and your neighbor as yourself.
—Luke 10:27

CHAPTER 8

The Work of the Holy Spirit

No one has seen the Holy Spirit, hence the need to use symbols and emblems to reveal the Holy Spirit.

In the same vein, the work of the Holy Spirit also reveals the presence of the Holy Spirit, or, as we rightly say, the presence of God. The more you know the work of the Holy Spirit, the better you'll know the Holy Spirit and understand Him and the things of God. And the more you know of the work of the Holy Spirit, the more you will let go and let God (Holy Spirit) work in your life to bring the necessary changes you are praying for.

Hosea 4:6a says, "My people are destroyed for lack of knowledge." Many Christians, as well as unbelievers, are in danger of committing the unpardonable *sin* against the Holy Spirit, only because of lack of knowledge. Too many people don't understand the manifestation of the Holy Spirit, so when they observe the moving of the Holy Spirit they misinterpret the manifestation and conclude that it is not of God. Some are even bold to say it is an evil spirit when, in fact, the Holy Spirit is at work.

Luke 12:10 warns that, "Anyone who speaks a word against the son of man, it will be forgiven, but to him who blasphemes against the Holy Spirit, it will not be forgiven." And Mark 3:29

emphasizes this fearful warning, saying, "But he who blasphemes against the Holy Spirit never has forgiveness but is subject to eternal condemnation."

These warnings make it imperative for those who judge the manifestation of the Holy Spirit to be extremely cautious.

What Is the Work of the Holy Spirit?

The Bible is full of the works of the Holy Spirit. From Genesis in the creative moments to Revelation at the consummation of God's plan, the Holy Spirit is at work. The author has attempted to discuss some of the works of the Holy Spirit. It is by no means exhaustive. Bear in mind that God is a Spirit, so the work of the Holy Spirit is the work of God, and the work of God is limitless. God said in Jeremiah 32:27, "Behold, I am the Lord, the God of all flesh, is there anything too hard for me?" Again, apostle Matthew in Matthew 19:26 declares, "But Jesus looked at them and said to them, 'With men this is impossible, but with God all things are possible.'" Here the Lord Jesus declares that what God can do is limitless. He is omnipotent and Almighty.

He is the Helper

John 16:7: "Nevertheless I tell you the truth. It is to your advantage that I go away; for if I do not go away the Helper will not come to you, but if I depart, I will send Him to you."

He Convicts Sinners

John 16:8–11: "And when He has come, He will convict the world of sin, and of righteousness, and of judgment, of sin, because they do not believe in me, of righteousness because I go to my Father and you see me no more; of judgment, because the ruler of this world is judged."

He Guides

John 16:13 states: "However, when He, the Spirit of Truth, has come, He will guide you into all truth; for He will not speak on His own authority, but whatever He hears He will speak; and He will tell you things to come."

He is the Glorifier

John 16:14: "He will glorify me, for He will take of what is mine and declare it to you."

He Helps the Believer to Pray Effectively

Romans 8:26 says: "Likewise the Spirit also helps in our weaknesses. For we do not know what we should pray for as we ought, but the Spirit Himself makes intercession for us with groanings which cannot be uttered."

Other activities of the Holy Spirit, to mention only a few, include the following.

The Holy Spirit Inspired the Writing of the Holy Bible

Second Peter 1:21 states: "For the prophecy never came by the will of man, but holy men of God spoke as they were moved by the Holy Spirit."

He Regenerates

John 3:5–6 says, "Jesus answered, 'Most assuredly I say to you, unless one is born of water and the Spirit, he cannot enter the kingdom of God. That which is born of the flesh is flesh, and that which is born of the Spirit is Spirit.'"

He brings newness to your life when you are born again of water and the Spirit. It is a renewal of mind, soul, body, and heart so you can think differently, act differently, and follow Jesus Christ.

Second Corinthians 5:17 states: "Therefore, if anyone is in Christ, he is a new creation; old things have passed away; behold, all things have become new."

He Sanctifies

Acts 13:2 also tells us, as they ministered to the Lord and fasted, the Holy Spirit said, "Now separate to me Barnabas and Saul for the work to which I have called them." That is sanctification, to be set apart for the work and glory of God.

He Leads

He leads the believer Romans 8:14: "As many as are led by the Spirit, they are the sons of God."

He Is a Reminder

John 14:26 reveals that He is our reminder. This is very obvious when a Christian is really upset. The Holy Spirit will tell you in a still small voice to be slow to anger and slow to talk, and when you are in deep problems He will remind you, to be still and know that He is God. When you are frightened He will remind you that, "Surely goodness and mercy shall follow you all the days of your life." When you are fearful and enemies come up against you, the Holy Spirit will remind you "Though you walk through the valley of the shadow of death … you should not be afraid because I'm with you. Remember, I'll never leave you nor forsake you." He is the reminder, He will remind you of the promises of God to strengthen you and increase your faith to move the many mountains that you'll encounter in your walk with the Lord.

He Is a Teacher

John 16:13 reveals that He is a teacher and the revealer of the future. The Holy Spirit is the Spirit of Prophecy. He is the Alpha and Omega, the Beginning and the End. He is God. In every instance and in every situation He is our guide, to remind us, to show us what to do and to teach us. If you the believer would allow the Holy Spirit to lead you, you will avoid many stumblings. By now you can see that there are many sides to the Holy Spirit.

So let's move on to greater things, for eyes have not seen, nor ears heard, nor has it entered into the heart of men what great things God has in store for those who love Him. The Holy Spirit anoints, illuminates, and directs the believer and the New Testament church. He empowers and enables the believer. He imparts Spiritual gifts to the believer and He assures the inner-man (the believer's soul) of salvation, crying Abba, Father.

Romans 8:15 says, "For you did not receive the spirit of bondage again to fear, but you received the Spirit of adoption by whom we cry out, Abba, Father."

And He is More

Dear friend,

This is an opportunity to understand the exciting principle of God. Take note that God is *Almighty.* All things are possible with Him. So He enables you to do all things through Christ (i.e., the Holy Spirit anointing *power* of God) who gives you strength. So all you need is to be filled with the Holy Spirit and all power in heaven and on earth is with you always.

Oh what a blessedness that we who were dead in our sins are now alive, cleansed by the precious blood of the Lord Jesus, and empowered by His almighty Holy Spirit, enabling us to do all things to the praise and glory of God.

CHAPTER 9

Add to Your Faith, "Arête" ("Virtue")

Looking at the contemporary Christian movement, with all the gossip, betrayals, lies, hypocrisy, avarice, and malice, it is evident that 2 Peter 1:5 is trampled, whereas 2 Timothy 3:1–7 reigns supreme.

Second Peter 1:5 instructs the believer, "Giving all diligence, add to your faith, virtue, and to virtue knowledge." It seems as if believers of today know only about faith, and faith has become an end in itself. But there is more that God desires to add to your faith. So prepare yourself to increase your knowledge, faith and anointing.

Arête is the Greek word for "virtue." Virtue may be defined, in theological context, as moral excellence and righteousness. A particularly efficacious, good and beneficial quality or advantage of a person or object. An effective force or power such as believing in the virtue of prayer.

Speaking of virtues to the Galatian believers, the apostle Paul defines virtue as Holy trait or characteristic of the believer produced by the indwelling Holy Spirit. In Galatians 5:22, the apostle metaphorically uses the word fruit (*karpos*) to mean virtue and proceeds to enumerate nine powerful Godly and Christ-like virtues to be manifested by all true believers. The indwelling

Holy Spirit is the intrinsic invisible power who produces the fruit (virtues) of the Holy Spirit in the believer.

These virtues, collectively and metaphorically grouped as "the fruit of the Spirit," are expected to be manifested by all believers as "Christian virtues."

Galatians 5:22–23 reveals that, "The fruits of the Spirit are love, joy, peace, longsuffering, kindness, goodness, faithfulness, gentleness, self-control; against such there is no law."

These characteristics are the holy traits of God produced in the believer by the Holy Spirit. The fruit of the Spirit may be defined as the supernatural grace, virtue, or divine characteristic of the Holy Spirit produced in and manifested by a believer to grow, live with and mature in the unity of the Holy Spirit as a disciple of the Lord Jesus Christ.

For better understanding, clarification, and easy application, the author has classified these virtues into three categories and groups of three per category.

Category 1

This is the believer's holy state of mind and attitude toward God and applied to other believers. These include, love, joy, and peace. These powerful holy traits are manifested through the believer's love of God (reverence of Jehovah), joy in the Holy Spirit (praise and worship of God), and peace with God (faith, respect, honor, and utmost fear of God, which produces wisdom in the believer).

The believer is required to extend these Holy traits to other believers.

Agape is the Greek word for "love." The agape type of love is the godly type, which must be differentiated from natural love

(Phileo and Eros). Agape may be defined as the love of choice or unconditional Love. This is the type of love God extends to the world and to believers. According to John 3:16: "For God so loved the world that He gave His only begotten Son that whoever believes in Him shall not perish but have everlasting life."

The same is manifested by the Lord Jesus Christ. No one has greater love than he who chose to lay down his life unconditionally for his friends.

Of faith, hope and love, the greatest is love. A full treatise on love is given in 1 Corinthians 13:1–13: Indeed 1 John 4:7, 20 also states, "Beloved, let us love one another, for love is of God, and everyone who loves is born of God and knows God. If someone says, 'I love God' and hates his brother, he is a liar, for he who does not love his brother whom he has seen, how can he love God whom he has not seen."

The Holy Spirit births the agape type of love in the believer, who is expected to expressly extend this same type of love to other believers. The believer is commanded to, "Love one another." It is not an option, it is a command, so let us obey and love one another.

Chara is the Greek word for "joy, delight or gladness." In Romans 14:17 we learn more of the kingdom of God, of which apostle Paul reveals "The kingdom of God is not about eating and drinking, but righteousness, and peace and joy in the Holy Spirit" (NIV).

This is another Christian virtue that passes all understanding when perceived also from the viewpoint of apostle James. James 1:2–3 counsels the believer to count it all as joy when you fall into various trials. These trials are designed to yield more virtues to bring the believer to the next higher level of maturity. After all, all things work together for good to those who love the

Lord. Rejoice and have joy within yourself. Why? Because God almighty is working it out for you and surely only goodness and mercy shall follow you all the days of your life, says the Good Shepherd.

Shalom is the Hebrew word for "peace." This is a state of well-being while maintaining the right relationship with God and keeping loving and peaceful harmony with other believers even in the midst of trials and adverse circumstances. This is the peace of God, which surpasses all understanding, that takes care of the believer's heart and mind in all circumstances.

Category 2

This is the horizontal social attitude or virtues toward other believers. These include *longsuffering* (patience), kindness, and goodness.

Makrothumia, the Greek word for longsuffering or patience, has the connotation of learning to not be easily offended. I call it "developing a thick skin" to other believers' irritants.

The truth is, believers are not perfect and take a long time to "grow up" in the Lord. So patience is the ability or quality of being able to put up with other people. This is not easy and you know it, but James 1:2–3 teaches that many trials are the design that develops the virtue of patience. So keep trying; you are almost there.

Kindness is a virtue that apostle Paul in Ephesians 4:32 admonishes the believer to exercise toward one another. "Be kind to one another," he declares. It is also another horizontal virtue so very much necessary that Colossians 3:12 counsels the believer to clothe himself with kindness.

Agathōsunē is the Greek word for goodness, a godly characteristic produced in the believer by the Holy Spirit. It is also a horizontal virtue, which causes the believer to be generous, gracious, and considerate toward others.

Category 3

This is the believer's conduct or characteristics about himself or herself. These include faithfulness, gentleness, and self-control.

Faithfulness is the state of being full of faith continuously. It is a quality of being worthy of trust, reliable, and loyal to a person (Jesus), a cause (salvation), and an idea (the gospel of the Lord Jesus Christ). Faithfulness simply says that the believer is rooted, grounded, unmovable, and unshakable, always abounding in the work of the Lord (1 Corinthians 15:58).

Prautés is the Greek word for gentleness, or meekness. I see a wonderful and beautiful situation here. Look at the almighty God with all power to make, break, or destroy, yet He is so gentle in His dealings with fragile human beings.

The Holy Spirit produces this fruit (virtue) in the believer to be humble and considerate, showing mercy and being gentle toward others.

Apostle Paul admonishes believers in Titus 3:2: "Speak evil of no one, to be peaceable, gentle, showing all humility to all men."

Indeed in 2 Corinthians 10:1, Paul declares, "Now, I, Paul, myself am pleading with you by the meekness and gentleness of Christ."

James 3:17 declares, "The wisdom that is from above is first pure, then peaceable, gentle, willing to yield, full of mercy and good fruits, without partiality and without hypocrisy." Beloved, let us be gentle toward one another.

Enkrateia is the Greek word for self-control, or temperance. Self-control simply says to take control of yourself. It is the quality of having mastery over your desires and passions. This is the much needed virtue of Christian discipline. The lack of it is the result of Christian incontinence and chaos in churches.

James 1:13–15 reveal the genesis of how lack of self control proceeds to self destruction. "Let no one say when he is tempted, I am tempted by God; for God cannot be tempted by evil, or does He Himself tempt anyone. But each one is tempted when he is drawn away by his own desires and enticed. Then, when desire has conceived, it gives birth to sin; and sin, when it is full grown, brings forth death."

This is the quality Paul speaks of in 1 Corinthians 9:27, saying, "I discipline my body and bring it into subjection." It is incumbent on all believers to be self-disciplined to become good soldiers in the army of God.

The author declares that it is all right to abound in the gifts of the Holy Spirit, but it is long overdue for every believer to earnestly desire to manifest the virtues (fruit) of the Holy Spirit.

The fruit of the Spirit are the essential ingredients (just like the essential amino acids needed for the healthy growth of a person) needed for a loving, joyful, and peaceful coexistence in the kingdom of God, down to your local church or prayer group and family level. You can do all things through Christ who strengthens you to bear and manifest the fruit of the Holy Spirit in your daily life to the praise and glory of God.

CHAPTER 10

Pneumatikos Charismata

The Greek word for Spirit is *pneuma*. It also means "wind or breath." The Greek word *pneumatikos* means spirituals.

The Greek word *charismata* means gifts of grace, from the singular charisma. Therefore, pneumatikos charistmata means, "Spiritual gifts of grace or gifts from the Holy Spirit. It is translated into current English as, "Gifts of the Holy Spirit." A Holy Spirit gift is a special supernatural enablement or ability or empowerment imparted to the believer by The Holy Spirit. The gift is also activated by the Holy Spirit. The gifts are given to believers filled with and baptized in the Holy Spirit as the Holy Spirit wills.

These gifts are given to believers as spiritual abilities to do the work of the Lord among believers and unbelievers. Hence, apostle Paul declares in 1 Corinthians 12:7, "But the manifestation of the Spirit is given to each one for the profit of all." This means the Holy Spirit gives a believer a spiritual gift to be used for the benefit and edification of all believers and unbelievers to the glory of God in the name of Jesus.

The gospel of the Lord Jesus Christ today, as in the days of old, needs to have signs and wonders to be fully and effectively preached, otherwise it will be relegated to the realm of the wisdom of men and not with the demonstration of the Spirit and with power. The apostle Paul reveals in 1 Corinthians 2:4–5, "My speech and my preaching were not with persuasive words of human wisdom but in demonstration of the Spirit and of power that your faith should not be in the wisdom of man but in the power of God."

Also, in Mark 16:20, the Bible states that they went out and preached everywhere, the Lord working with them and confirming the word through accompanying signs. Again in Hebrews 2:4, it is stated, "God also bearing witness both with signs and wonders, with various miracles and gifts of the Holy Spirit according to His own will."

Therefore, let it be emphasized that the gospel of the Lord Jesus Christ as in the days of old needs to have signs, wonders, miracles, which are gifts of the Holy Spirit following to be fully and effectively preached. It is the gospel of power or anointing. The Holy Spirit gives these gifts to the believer according to His will.

A believer of God is not to be ignorant of the Spirit that he or she has received from God. The apostle Paul reveals in 1 Corinthians 12:1–11,

> Now concerning spiritual gifts, brethren, I do not want you to be ignorant: **y**ou know that you were Gentiles, carried away to these dumb idols, however you were led. Therefore, I make known to you that no one speaking by the Spirit of God calls Jesus accursed and no one can say that Jesus is Lord except by the Holy Spirit. There are diversities of gifts, but the same Spirit. There are differences of ministries but the same Lord. And

there are diversities of activities, but is the same God that works all in all. But the manifestation of the Spirit is given to each one for the profit of all. For to one is given the word of wisdom through the Spirit, to another the word of knowledge through the same Spirit. To another faith by the same Spirit to another gifts of healing by the same Spirit. To another the working of miracles, to another prophecy, to another discerning of Spirits, to another different kinds of tongues, to another the interpretation of tongues. But one and the same Spirit works all these things, distributing to each one individually as He wills.

It is obvious that the church of the Corinthians were unlearned about the gifts of the Spirit; subsequently, the manifestation of the Spirit as well as the diversity of the gifts and the different activities by the Holy Spirit through the individuals in the church created no small confusion.

Hosea 4:6 states, "My people are destroyed for lack of knowledge." Here it is obvious the lack of knowledge and understanding among the Corinthians resulted in the obvious misuse and misinterpretation of the Holy Spirit activities. Nevertheless, it is clearly explained in 1 Corinthians 12:3–6.

The word *diversities*, which seems to cause confusion, simply means different kinds of. Therefore, verse 4 reads like this: "There are different kinds of gifts but all these different kinds of gifts are given by the same Holy Spirit."

This reveals the omnipotence of the Holy Spirit, in that however big the problem seems to be, the Holy Spirit has the anointing power to deal with it through the gift.

Verse 5 states, "There are differences of ministries, but the same Lord." The important thing to observe is differences of ministries. Here the understanding is that, the different gifts all come from the greatest gift, which is the Holy Spirit and the ministries are fashioned by the main minister who is the Lord Jesus Christ. So in verse five we see that the Lord Jesus Christ by His Holy Spirit gives gifts to various ministers in the ministry according to what He desires to minister. Hence the different kinds of ministries. This also explains the fivefold ministry offices. According to the measure of gifts and anointing given to a person by the Holy Spirit, this person is ushered into the apostolic, prophetic, pastoral, evangelistic, or teaching ministry.

This also is confirmed in Ephesians 4:7, which states, "But to each one of us grace was given according to Christ's gift."

First Corinthians 12:6 explains, "And there are diversities of activities, but it is the same God who works all in all."

In this verse we see various kinds of activities, but it is clear that it is the same God who is working by His Spirit through individuals and in different ministers.

First Corinthians 12:7 explains, "But the manifestation of the Spirit is given to each one for the profit of all."

This clearly identifies a spiritual gift as a supernatural ability given to an individual by the Holy Spirit to be manifested, which means to give visible evidence of the active work of the Holy Spirit through the individual with a view that the entire church body will benefit seeing, realizing, and experiencing the presence of God as manifested.

Now let us look at First Corinthians 12:8–10. "For to one is given the word of wisdom through the Spirit, to another the word of knowledge through the same Spirit, to another faith by the same Spirit, to another gifts of healing by the same Spirit, to another the working of miracles, to another prophecy, to another discerning of spirits, to another different kinds of tongues, to another the interpretation of tongues."

A closer look at this Scripture reveals that, to one person and to another and to various individuals, the Holy Spirit gives these gifts. So in a church among true believers some will speak in tongues, some will interpret, some will heal, and some will prophesy according to how the Holy Spirit gives the gifts to the individuals in the church.

All may or may not speak in tongues, and all may or may not prophesy, because the Holy Spirit distributes the gifts to the believers in the church and each person's gift, as different as it may be, is meant to edify the entire church body. The Holy Spirit gives every believer a gift, but it's not what you want, it is according to what the purpose of God or the will of God is for your calling.

It is not necessary that all Christians have the same gift. Why? Because each person's gift is for the benefit of all in the congregation. The manifestation of all the gifts make up the total body of Christ in the church, just as the different parts of the human body make up the complete person. Therefore, it is necessary for a church to strive for all the different kinds of gifts.

Let us take a closer look at 1 Corinthians 12:29–30 "Are all apostles? Are all prophets? Are all teachers? Are all workers of miracles?" "Do all have gifts of healing? Do all speak with tongues? Do all interpret?" Here it is very clear that the Holy Spirit does not make everyone an apostle or prophet, nor is everyone a teacher, nor do all have the gift of healing. Therefore, it is easily possible that all may speak in tongues, but in reality, not all speak in tongues. The Holy Spirit may give other gifts to those who do not speak in tongues and their gifts are also for edification.

Similarly, all may interpret tongues, but in reality, not all believers interpret tongues. The Holy Spirit may give them other gifts for edification. Note the miracle and beauty as well as the mystery of God that the entire human body is not made of one nose or one hand but is made up of different parts to produce one beautiful or handsome person to the praise and glory of God.

Let me share a few revelations with you.

- Reading and finding out about the gifts of the Holy Spirit does not mean you must have all the gifts, though you may desire all the gifts. The Christian must remember that, all too often, it is what *we want*, forgetting that it is God who called us according to His purpose and will.

- When God called the believer by His Son, Jesus Christ, He had a purpose in His mind for you. Romans 8:28 says, "To those who are called according to his purpose." Now therefore, according to the purpose that God has for your calling the Holy Spirit of God will give you the exact spiritual gift or gifts that you need to accomplish God's purpose in you.

- Many times the child of God will be trying to heal when your gift is to prophesy, or burning your brains out to speak in tongues when the Holy Spirit is preparing you to interpret the tongues being spoken by other believers. Believers need to stand still to know the will of God for your life or calling which determines the gift(s) the Holy Spirit shall give you as He wills.

- Remember, God by His grace and mercy has called you by His Son, Jesus Christ, and God knows exactly what He called you for, so be patient and wait on the Lord as He gives us progressive revelation concerning the purpose of your calling. He who called you will also equip you with the appropriate gift(s) to do the work for Him and for His glory.

There are many gifts of the Holy Spirit revealed to the believer. I encourage you to always remember that the revealed things of the Lord belong to the believers. So receive and use the gifts to the glory of God in the name of Jesus.

A comprehensive list of the gifts of the Holy Spirit can be found in the Holy Bible. However, for clarity the author has classified them in two broad and major categories, Old Testament Holy Spirit gifts and New Testament Holy Spirit gifts.

The Old Testament Holy Spirit Gifts

These include

- prophecy, revealed through all the prophets
- miracles done by the prophets attest to this Holy Spirit gift
- faith, seen in all the Old Testament men and women of faith
- healing, especially by prophets Moses, Elijah, Elisha, and Isaiah
- knowledge (Daniel 5:12)
- understanding (Daniel 5:12)
- interpretation of dreams (Daniel 5:12)
- solving riddles (Daniel 5:12)
- explaining enigmas (Daniel 5:12)
- wisdom (Deuteronomy 34:9; 1 Kings 4:29)

- government (Genesis. 42:6; 1 Samuel 16:1–13; Psalm 22:28)
- teaching—Almost all the Old Testament prophets had the gift of teaching.
- helps (ministering)—All the Old Testament priests had this gift.
- exhortation—revealed by all the exhortations of the prophets to Israel
- giving is expressly manifest in the church in the wilderness despite their major shortcomings
- pasturing—Most of the major prophets were the pastors of Israel.

The New Testament Holy Spirit Gifts

Romans 12:6–8

- prophecy
- ministration
- teaching
- exhortation
- giving
- leadership (government)
- showing mercy

1 Corinthians 12:8–10

- word of wisdom
- word of knowledge
- healing

- working of miracles
- prophecy
- faith
- discerning of spirits
- tongues
- interpretation of tongues

1 Corinthians 12:28–30

- apostleship
- prophet
- teaching
- workers of miracles
- healing
- helps (ministrations)
- administrations
- varieties of tongues

Ephesians 4:11

- apostleship
- prophecy
- evangelism
- pastoring
- teaching

For clarity, the author has grouped the New Testament Holy Spirit gifts into four categories.

The Gifts of the Holy Spirit

1. Revelation Gifts

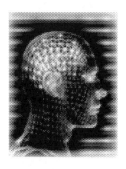

- word of wisdom
- word of knowledge
- discerning of the Spirit

2. Power Gifts

- healing
- working of miracles
- faith

3. Speaking Gifts

- apostleship
- prophecies, pastoring, teaching, exhortation
- tongues
- interpretation of tongues

4. Governing, Ministering, or Serving Gifts

- government (leadership)
- helps (ministration)
- hospitality
- giving
- showing mercy

Definitions and Comparisons

To answer the many questions I have received on this and related subjects, the author offers the following definitions and comparison of gifts, fruits, and the natural endowment referred to as talent.

Gift of the Holy Spirit: a special supernatural or divine enablement or ability or empowerment imparted to the believer by the Holy Spirit.

Fruit of the Holy Spirit: a supernatural grace, or divine characteristic of the Holy Spirit produced in and manifested by a believer to grow, live with and mature in the unity of the Holy Spirit as disciples of the Lord Jesus.

Talent: a natural endowment of a person. A special, often creative or artistic aptitude, also a general intelligence, mental acuity or power of a person, according to Merriam Webster's Collegiate Dictionary, Tenth Edition.

<u>Comparison</u>

Gifts	Fruit	Talent
Supernatural grace from Holy Spirit of God. Given at Holy Spirit infilling (baptism). Spiritual empowerment of the believer. For believers spiritual growth and Christian service.	Divine Characteristic from Holy Spirit of God Available at Holy Spirit baptism. Spiritual qualities of the believer. For believers' peaceful spiritual and social life.	Natural grace of the soul of man. Present at natural birth. Natural ability of a person can be learned as an acquired ability. For educational instruction entertainment, inspiration at a natural level.
This is what a believer has received from the Holy Spirit for service or for the work of the Lord.	This deals with character of believer (love, joy, peace, goodness, kindness, etc.). This is what the believer has or can become for now and eternity.	This deals with developing a person's own natural abilities.

What Are the Gifts of the Holy Spirit For?

First Corinthians 12:7 declares, "But the manifestation of the Spirit is given to each one for the profit of all."

Here we see the major purpose of the gifts of the Holy Spirit: "For the profit of all." This means the gift of the Holy Spirit is given to a believer not for vainglory but to use the gifts to benefit everyone and for the greater good of all people. For example, the gift of tongues is to benefit unbelievers as well as to edify the speaker. The interpretation of tongues benefits all those who hear it. The gift of healing benefits all who are oppressed with sicknesses. The miracle gift of casting out demons is to benefit and set free all who are oppressed, suppressed and possessed by demons or evil spirits. The gift of wisdom and word of knowledge are all invaluable in the congregation. It is evident that the gifts of the Holy Spirit are truly given to each believer to edify everyone.

First Corinthians 12:27 also states, "Now you are the body of Christ and members individually." This introduces another purpose of the Holy Spirit gifts. This is to form an effective dynamic fruit-bearing body or local church.

The apostle Paul effectively uses the "body concept" of a person as an analogy to the "Body of Christ." The apostle Paul in 1 Corinthians 12:14 eloquently portrays the body as being made up of many gifted parts, and each part performs or uses its gifts to benefit the entire human body.

For example, the eyes see for the entire person, the brain thinks for the entire person, the legs walk for the entire person, the mouth speaks for the entire person, and the heart beats for the entire person. In the same way, the believer with the gift of healing uses the gift to heal every sick person in the congregation (known as the body of Jesus Christ). The one who interprets tongues does it for the benefit of everyone. The one who prophesies does so for the benefit of the entire body of Christ, and the one with the gift of miracles uses this gift to benefit the entire congregation.

Therefore, the use of all the gifts of the Holy Spirit, just like the use of all the human body parts, collectively make up and build or edify the entire body of Jesus Christ. In a church where the gifts are suppressed, there are often so many sick people (referred to as shut-ins), and faith is always at its lowest ebb, The church remains paralyzed and the Bible refers to such a church as "having a form of godliness but without power." So, believer, stir up your gift and use it to benefit your church and for the glory of God.

Finally, let us think of the gifts this way: every gift of the Holy Spirit is for the exact work that the gift is named. Examine the gift of wisdom.

When all believers receive the gift of wisdom, much confusion, strife, gossip, anger, jealousy, and malice among Christians will abate. When the gift of healing is stirred up, so many sick people in the church will be healed by the use of this gift. Some things in your life will not change unless you get a miracle. That is why God has given the church the gift of working miracles. The gifts of help, administration, and the rest are all given to individuals in the church for the work of the ministry.

Are the Holy Spirit Gifts for Today's Church?

There are those who believe the gifts of the Holy Spirit ceased soon after the first-generation apostles of the Lord Jesus. Some even contend that the gifts are not needed or necessary for the present generation. I call this concept the "Devil's deception." Let us destroy and dispel this concept of unbelief immediately with the following swords of the Spirit.

1. The Holy Bible commands you not to be *ignorant* of the gifts of the Holy Spirit. First Corinthians 12:1 says, "Now concerning spiritual gifts, brethren, I do not want you to be ignorant." Notice that the Devil, our adversary, would like to keep us ignorant. But Lucifer was, is, and forever will be a liar! Let the believer study to show yourself approved unto God and not to the propagators of the doctrine of lies and deception.

2. You are commanded to *not* neglect your gifts in 1 Timothy 4:14.

3. You are commanded *to stir up* the gifts in 2 Timothy 1:6.

Notice that even if the gifts have ceased or lay dormant, the word of God commands us to revive them and stir them into activity in this generation. And that is exactly what God is doing in the churches these last days. It's Pentecost all over again. Do not the let latter rain pass you by!

4. The believer is commanded to earnestly desire spiritual gifts (see 1 Corinthians 12:31).

5. The Lord Jesus personally listed some of the supernatural gifts, which are the credentials of the believers (Mark 16:17–18).

6. Mark 16:19–20 reveals that the gospel of the Lord Jesus Christ needs "signs and wonders" to follow to be fully and effectively propagated.

7. Finally, apostle Paul reveals that gifted and anointed offices are given to the New Testament churches as in Ephesians

4:11–12: "And He Himself gave some to be apostles, some prophets, some evangelists, and some pastors and teachers, for the equipping of the saints for the work of ministry, for the edifying of the body of Christ."

Bear in mind that just as there were generational prophets in the Old Testament days, so also the Lord Jesus Christ continues to appoint generational apostles for the sixth dispensation. This is the dispensation of the fivefold ministry offices. The above is sufficient to instruct the reader that the gifts are needed today and right now in your local church.

They are needed to heal, cast-out demons, to deliver, set free, and save souls, and to build the kingdom of God in the name of Jesus.

It is obvious that the believer cannot do the works that the Lord Jesus did and do greater works without the power, anointing, and gifts of the Holy Spirit.

First Corinthians 12:28 states: "And God has appointed these in the church: first apostle, second prophets, third teachers, miracles, then gifts of healings, helps, administrations, varieties of tongues."

God appoints all these gifts in the church of today. They are needed. Claim these gifts for your local church and be on fire for Jesus.

Until the work of the ministry is fully completed, all the demons and witches are cast out. The body of Christ is fully built up to maturity, and the saints come to the unity of the faith. The knowledge of the Son of God, to a perfect man and to the measure of the stature of the fullness of Christ all the Holy Spirit gifts and ministry offices are needed in every church everywhere.

So keep casting demons out, healing, speaking and praying in tongues, interpreting tongues, and prophesying with signs and wonders. All the gifts are needed now in your church.

Finally, to say the gifts of the Holy Spirit have ceased is to say God has ceased baptizing Christians with the Holy Spirit.

The truth is, God is still baptizing all who are being saved in the name of Jesus and the Holy Spirit is never without His power, gifts and fruits. So all believers that are being filled and baptized with the Holy Spirit are still receiving the gifts of the Holy Spirit with the requisite anointing. You owe it to yourself to believe and receive your anointing.

Apostle Peter explains in Acts 2:17–18, 21, "These are not drunk as you suppose but this is what was spoken by the prophet Joel."

Acts 2:17–18: "And it shall come to pass in the last days, says God, That I will pour out of My Spirit on all flesh; Your sons and your daughters shall prophesy, your young men shall see visions, your old men shall dream dreams. And on my menservants and on my maidservants I will pour out my Spirit in those days; and they shall prophesy."

Acts 2:21: "And it shall come to pass that whoever calls on the name of the Lord shall be saved."

It is revealed here that there will be an outpouring of the Holy Spirit upon all flesh, young and old, and upon all genders and races. It is also revealed that the outpouring will come with additional Holy Spirit supernatural gifts, such as

- the gift of prophecy (sons and daughters)
- the gift of visions (young men)
- the gift is supernatural revelation in dreams (old men)

Menservants and maidservants shall also prophesy. The prophecy also came with the grace of God in Acts 2:21, which says, "Whoever calls on the name of the Lord shall be saved."

There is so much attention drawn to the outpouring of the Holy Spirit on all flesh on the day of Pentecost, and this is true. I believe that we have a great opportunity here to claim all God's promises concerning the gifts prophesied in Joel 2:28–29. The truth is, Satan is just happy to see that we have forgotten our gifts of prophecy, supernatural revelation in dreams, and young men with visions.

So, believer, it's that time again for us to go back to the throne of grace and pray and seek the Lord to claim our gifts of prophecy, that the Lord would grant our older believers the wonderful gift of supernatural revelation in dreams and that all our young men may avoid calamities by using their supernatural gift of seeing godly visions.

So what happened on the day of Pentecost? On this beautiful and sanctified day, Jehovah was again on–target, fulfilling His prophecies. There is a time and a season for all the plans of God. The day of Pentecost was the time and season to fulfill two major prophecies. The first was Joel 2:28–29, explained above.

The second was to fulfill the prophecy of Isaiah 28:11–12, referenced in 1 Corinthians 14:21: "With men of other tongues and other lips I will speak to this people; and yet, for all that, they will not hear me, says the Lord."

This is where God astonishes the nations that were gathered in Jerusalem with a special supernatural gift of utterance in tongues (unknown to the Galilean believers) to allow the unbelievers to hear, understand, believe, and call on the name of the Lord and be saved as prophesied in Joel 2:32. As God will have it, on this Holy day of prophetic fulfillment, the tongues in which the believers spoke as the Holy Spirit gave them utterance became a great and mighty sign to the unbelievers gathered from many nations. The Bible reveals that three thousand unbelievers called on the name of the Lord and were saved (Acts 2:21), baptized, and added to the kingdom of God (Acts 2:41).

CHAPTER 11

Glossolalia

The Greek word *glossolalia* means "speaking in tongues."

The word "tongue" is defined as a language or dialect. The plural is tongues, which means languages or dialects. It is a supernatural impartation to the believer by the Holy Spirit. It is also one of the speaking or utterance gifts of the Holy Spirit to the believer.

On the day of Pentecost, when the disciples were all filled with the Holy Spirit, they began to speak in other tongues as the Holy Spirit gave them utterance. The Bible reveals that these tongues were languages of other nations such as, Parthians, Medes, Elamites, Mesopotamia, Judea, Cappadocia, Pontus, Asia, Phrygia, Pamphylia, Egypt, Libya, Cyrene, Rome, Cretans, and Arabia.

Acts 2:8–11 enlightens us: "And how is it that we hear, in our own language in which we were born? Parthians, and Medes, and Elamites, those dwelling in Mesopotamia, Judea and Cappadocia, Pontus, Asia, Phrygia and Pamphylia, Egypt, and the parts of Libya adjoining Cyrene, visitors from Rome, both Jews and Proselytes, Cretans, and Arabs—we hear them speaking in our own tongues the wonderful works of God."

There are different types of languages or dialects. There are different categories of languages or dialects. For the above reasons, the Holy Bible groups the different types and categories as "diversities of tongues." This is one gift of the Holy Spirit that has generated so much controversy.

Why is there so much controversy? The following, I believe, are some of the reasons that may explain the controversy over the gift of tongues.

- It is not well taught in the churches, especially by those who do not believe in this gift.

- It is mysterious and exciting, and people do not understand it; some call the gift "ecstatic utterance" and others call it "babbling."

- The gift of interpretation of tongues is not much in operation, and not enough emphasis is placed on it compared to the "must speak in tongues" emphasis. So much of the unknown tongues spoken are not interpreted to edify the church.

- It is a New Testament experience, and many believers who have this gift have the erroneous belief they will arrive in heaven before other saints without the gift.

- Many believers and unbelievers alike do not take the time to study the proper use of this gift to edify the church. Hence its abuse and subsequent misuse, conflict, and confusion.

- Finally, it is because those who seem to understand this gift also come with mysterious assumptions to further complicate the issue without cognizance to other evidential gifts.

Let me add these points for clarity. Speaking in tongues is

- a New Testament experience different from all the old testament gifts of the Holy Spirit, even though it was prophesied in the Old Testament.
- one of the nine gifts of the Holy Spirit listed by the apostle Paul in 1 Corinthians 12. There are many other gifts of the Holy Spirit not listed in this chapter.
- one of the evidences of baptism of the Holy Spirit. It is by no means the only evidence of being baptized or filled with the Holy Spirit. This will be explained as you read on. Believers need to reclaim all the other gifts of the Holy Spirit that the Devil would like to steal from us.

For clarity, the author has grouped the gift of tongues into three categories: known tongues, unknown tongues, and mystery tongues.

Known Tongues

These are languages or dialects of other nations or people here on Earth. They are understood and interpreted by the nationals or people whose language or tongue is being spoken. (See Acts 2:8–11.)

These languages or tongues were never learned by the speaker, and that is why it is a supernatural gift to the speaker. However, these tongues can be interpreted by the speaker if the Holy Spirit gives the gift of interpretation to the speaker.

Unknown Tongues

These are Holy Spirit languages or utterances given to the believer. It may be interpreted by the speaker if the speaker has the gift of interpretation or could be interpreted by another believer who has the gift of interpretation of unknown tongues. These are languages not spoken here on earth and are therefore referred to as unknown tongues. These utterances could be God's message or prophecy to the world, country, city, church, or individual, hence the need for interpretation for edification for the greater good of everyone.

Mystery Tongues

First Corinthians 14:2 states, "He who speaks in a tongue does not speak to men but to God, for no one understands him; however, in the spirit he speaks mysteries."

These are unknown tongues of communication between the believer and God. These are not interpreted by the speaker or by another believer. These are mysteries spoken by the believer for the believer's own edification.

This is why the apostle Paul counsels that if a believer speaks in mystery tongues in the congregation and there is no interpretation, what the speaker is saying has no benefit to the congregation and therefore must limit the communication to the speaker and God alone. Note that it has great benefit to the speaker and thus cannot be forbidden.

Many have also categorized unknown and mystery tongues as the believer's prayer language. The Bible affirms that the believer can pray in the Spirit, which could also mean praying in tongues.

Clarification

Some argue that all the disciples spoke in other languages on the day of Pentecost, and Cornelius and his household spoke in tongues, so every new believer must speak in tongues. Let us see the prophecy on tongues revealed in 1 Corinthians 14:21–22: "In the law it is written, 'With men of other tongues and other lips I will speak to this people; and yet, for all that, they will not hear me,' says the Lord. 'Therefore, tongues are for a sign, not to those who believe but to the unbelievers; but prophesying is not for unbelievers but for those who believe.'"

The word *sign* is defined as an outward manifestation of a spiritual significance. Webster defines it as a discernible indication of what is not itself directly perceptible, a token. In the days of the Lord Jesus and thereafter the Pharisees, Sadducees, and scribes were unbelievably unbelieving. Their statement of faith would read something like, "Seeing is believing," or "I need a sign to believe."

Keep in mind that the Lord proclaimed in John 20:29, "Blessed are those who have not seen and yet have believed." This is the post-resurrection incidence, when the "doubting Thomas" of the twelve apostles would not believe the resurrection of the Lord Jesus unless he saw and touched the nail scars.

In Matthew 12:38, in a pre-crucifixion incidence, the unbelieving Pharisees and scribes demanded to see a sign from the Lord Jesus, prompting Him to call them an evil and adulterous generation seeking a sign. It is therefore evident that the Jewish skeptics and unbelievers would not believe anything unless they saw a sign. With this knowledge in mind, it is easy to understand why on the day of Pentecost God gave the sign of tongues (which were languages of other nations) to convince, convert, and save the unbelievers gathered in Jerusalem. The sign of other tongues did work the miracle of three thousand souls being saved.

After this, there was the need to eliminate prejudice and discrimination between the Jews and the gentiles. Prejudice, discrimination, and racism are hindrances to the effective propagation of the gospel.

Bear in mind that the apostles were accustomed to being sent to preach the gospel to the house of Israel only. They were thus prejudiced and considered the gospel for the Jews only. But now the Lord Jesus commanded them in the great commission to go to all nations. God, who always has solutions to our problems, had the answer ready to be revealed through apostle Peter, the Jew, and Cornelius, the Gentile. The occasion was organized by the Holy Spirit, who brought apostle Peter to the house of Cornelius.

Apostle Peter relates the account in Acts 10 and declared that God authenticated the true conversion of Cornelius, the Gentile, and his household with the baptism of the Holy Spirit evidenced by the gentiles speaking the same tongues that apostle Peter, the Jew, and others spoke on the day of Pentecost. Here, it is evident that God used speaking in tongues to convince the skeptical Jewish believers that the gospel was universal and that it was for the gentiles as well. Henceforth, there is no Jew or gentile in the Lord. Salvation is for all who will believe and accept Jesus as Lord and Savior.

God was not yet through with hindrances that still existed. Here was Saul, the persecutor of the believers. Suddenly he called himself Paul, after having undergone a spiritual metamorphosis, and preached the gospel he once fought against.

No one wanted to believe him, especially the skeptical Jewish believers. Again, God had the answer to give apostle Paul a breakthrough in his preaching of the gospel.

So at Ephesus, the Holy Spirit facilitated the conversion of the followers of John the Baptist with tongues and prophecy as evidence of the truthfulness of apostle Paul's calling and ministry. Again, we see God using speaking in other tongues to convince and convert the skeptical Jewish followers of the forerunner.

The author concludes that speaking in tongues is a sign for unbelievers and skeptics. In addition, according to the will and purpose of God, the Holy Spirit gives the believer the appropriate gifts as He wills. That is why it is not necessary for everyone to speak in other languages, although the Holy spirit could cause everyone to speak in tongues if it suits the will and purpose of God.

A closer examination of the following scriptures is very revealing indeed.

The apostles never preached that salvation is made by speaking in tongues. They preached the baptism of the Holy Spirit. The Holy Spirit is given to them who obey the Lord, and He, the Holy Spirit, imparts specific gifts to the believer as He will.

Acts 5:32 reveals, "And we are His witnesses to these things, so also is the Holy Spirit whom God has given to those who obey Him."

When Peter laid his hands on the baptized and they received the Holy Spirit, the Bible does not state that they spoke in tongues. We see in Acts 8:12–17,

> But when they believed Philip as he preached the things concerning the kingdom of God in the name of Jesus Christ, both men and women were baptized. Then Simon himself also believed; and when he was baptized he continued with Philip, and was amazed, seeing the miracles and signs,

> which were done. Now when the apostles who were at Jerusalem heard that Samaria had received the word of God, they sent Peter and John to them, who, when they had come down, prayed for them that they might receive the Holy Spirit. For as yet he had fallen upon none of them. They had only been baptized in the name of the Lord Jesus. Then they laid hands on them, and they received the Holy Spirit.

Please take note that you could be baptized in water and not have the Holy Spirit baptism.

When Paul was converted on his way to Damascus, it is not stated that he got up speaking in tongues. Instead, he spoke boldly with the Spirit and spoke in tongues later. Acts 9:20-22: "Immediately he preached the Christ in the synagogues, that He is the Son of God. Then all who heard, were amazed, and said, 'Is this not he who destroyed those who call on this name in Jerusalem, and has come here for that purpose, so that he might bring them bound to the chief priests? But Saul increased all the more in strength, and confounded the Jews who dwelled in Damascus, proving that Jesus is the Christ.'"

In Acts 9:29, we see, "And he spoke boldly in the name of the Lord Jesus and disputed against the hellenists, but they attempted to kill him."

The jailer was baptized, all his household did not speak in tongues, yet they were all saved. Acts 16:30–34: "And he brought them out and said, 'Sirs, what must I do to be saved?' So they said, 'Believe in the Lord Jesus Christ, and you will be saved, you and your household.' Then they spoke the word of the Lord to him and to all who were in his house, and he took them the same hour of the night and washed their stripes. And immediately he and all his family were baptized. Now when he had brought them into his house, he set food before them; and he rejoiced, having believed in God with all his household."

Tongues are a sign for unbelievers and skeptics. It is a supernatural gift from the Holy Spirit, which any believer can receive as the Holy Spirit gives (see 1 Corinthians 14:1–33).

God is sovereign and has many different ways of manifesting the presence of His Spirit as seen in 1 Corinthians 12:5–6. Anyone of the Holy Spirit gifts is a manifestation or an evidence of being filled and baptized with the Holy Spirit. For example, speaking in tongues is a classic New Testament evidence of the Holy Spirit baptism. But the interpretation of tongues is also a classic New Testament evidence of being filled and baptized with the Holy Spirit.

To prophesy is also an evidence of being baptized with the Holy Spirit because prophecy is also a powerful gift of the Holy Spirit listed in 1 Corinthians 12. Bear in mind that no one can manifest a gift of the Holy Spirit unless he or she is filled and baptized with the Holy Spirit. Why? Because the Holy Spirit is the only source of the gifts.

For every lock, there is a key. Speaking in unknown tongues is the lock and unless you have the key to unlock it, you will certainly be locked out of the meaning of what is said. But God gave us the key, and the key to unknown tongues is the gift of interpretation of tongues.

Believer, I want you to know that because God gave us a new gift called speaking in other tongues, He also has given us another New Testament gift known as interpretation of tongues to avail ourselves every bit of what God wants to bless us with no matter in what language it is spoken.

Summary

1. Manifestation of Holy Spirit gift is possible only when you are baptized with the Holy Spirit. Therefore, manifestation of any gift of the Holy Spirit is an evidence of being baptized with the Holy Spirit.

2 There are three new gifts in addition to all the other gifts for the New Testament believer. These are speaking in other tongues, interpretation of other tongues, and casting out demons in the name of Jesus Christ.

2. Speaking in unknown tongues is a classic New Testament evidence of being baptized with the Holy Spirit as a sign to convince and convert unbelievers and to edify the believer with this gift.

3. Interpretation of these unknown tongues to unlock spoken mysteries is also a classic New Testament evidence of being baptized with the Holy Spirit.

4. Casting out demons in the name of Jesus is also a classic New Testament evidence of being filled and baptized with the Holy Spirit. We know that the Devil does not cast himself out, and the name of Jesus Christ is used only in the New Testament.

5. Every believer must seek these gifts in addition to all the other gifts of the Holy Spirit, which are also evidences of being baptized with the Holy Spirit.

Henceforth, we shall not allow the confusionist, yes, that old Serpent, to deceive and cheat us of all our Holy Spirit gifts. These belong to the believer to empower him or her to do the work of the Lord. Therefore, earnestly desire all the gifts of the

Holy Spirit. It is the promise of God to you. Claim them all in the name of Jesus.

The believer must live by the fruits of the Holy Spirit and work the work of God by the Gifts of the Holy Spirit. Note that a believer can be filled and baptized with the Holy Spirit before water baptism, and in like manner a believer can be filled with the Holy Spirit and manifest other gifts and speak in tongues much later after Holy Spirit baptism.

There is yet another potent Holy Spirit gift that the Lord Jesus promised the believers in Acts 1:8: "But you shall receive power (dunamis) when the Holy Spirit has come upon you; and you shall be witnesses to Me in Jerusalem, and in all Judea and Samaria, and to the end of the earth."

This is the Holy Spirit power, which is the personal spiritual power (PSP), or anointing of the believer, and is needed by every believer to do the work of God and to witness unto Jesus Christ. Every believer who is baptized with the Holy Spirit can and must have the Holy Spirit power to witness unto the Lord Jesus Christ. It is the will of God to endue you with *power* from on high. The thing with believers these days is that everybody speaks in tongues and very few have power, so believers are riddled with problems of confusion, but God is not the author of confusion.

First Corinthians 14:33: "For God is not the author of confusion but of peace, as in all the churches of the saints." Everybody speaks in tongues, but few are casting the witches and demons out. Everybody speaks in tongues, but most practice separation, prejudice, racism, and better-than-thou behavior in the churches that tend to create division among Christians, thereby weakening the Christian movement because a house divided amongst itself cannot stand.

Everybody speaks in tongues, but most turn around to speak lies, gossip, and practice malice against their brothers and sisters. Everybody speaks in tongues so much that almost no one is cleansing the church of the holier-than-thou folks. Everyone speaks in tongues, and few are healing and almost no one interprets either.

Everyone speaks in tongues, but most Christians have a hard time loving one another. Obviously all the gifts and ministries are needed to build a wholesome ministry even as revealed in 1 Corinthians 12:27–28: "Now you are the body of Christ and member individually. God has appointed these in the church: first, apostles; second, prophets; third, teachers, miracles, gifts of healing, helps, administration, varieties of tongues."

I hasten to add that the Lord Jesus Christ has yet more to say about other manifestations of the Holy Spirit in a believer. Mark 16:17–18: "And these signs shall follow those who believe: In my name they shall cast out demons,   speak with new tongues, take up serpents, drink any deadly thing, it shall not hurt them; lay hands on the sick and they shall recover."

These are essential supernatural credentials of a New Testament believer, prescribed by the founder of the New Testament Church, the Lord Jesus Christ. These words from the Lord Jesus require that we speak in tongues, but in addition, God has given us believers power to cast out demons, take up serpents, and lay hands on the sick and pray for their healing. It seems to me that the Devil wants to steal some of our gifts, but the Devil is a liar.

Believer, enjoy the gift of speaking in tongues, however, let us move on to other areas such as laying hands on the sick and heal them as well as winning souls for the Kingdom of God. It is clear, dear reader that *the Christian's only means of survival* is *revival*. So rise up with a new understanding of the Holy Spirit in you and pick up the sword (the word of God) by the *renewing* of your *mind* and let us go and fight a good fight like well trained intelligent and wise soldiers of the Lord. It is about time Christians understood their God and join the Battalion for Jesus. Yes, every one of you precious children of God, I challenge you to stand up for Jesus. Cast out petty confusion and join ranks to march like a strong army against the enemy at all fronts to overcome and conquer. Victory is ours in the name of Jesus.

Undue preoccupation with speaking in tongues only, is a clear and valid indication of spiritual childishness. First Corinthians 14:19–20. We need to claim and use all the other Holy Spirit gifts that God has promised us.

Every gift is an anointing for the believer. Think of how much anointing we lose when we do not use all of our gifts. The universal promise for every believer in Acts 1:8, "But you shall receive power after the Holy Spirit is come upon you," is crucial in these last days of multiplication of evil and wickedness.

This promise is an important, necessary anointing power for all the Nebuchadnezzar fires you will go through, all the rivers and oceans you will cross, and all the valleys and mountains you will encounter while following the Lord Jesus on your way to the new Canaan, which is heaven.

The question is, have you received this anointing? Are you endued with Holy Spirit *power* from on High?

For example, the Lord Jesus Christ sent out seventy and the twelve with power (anointing) and whereas they did not speak in tongues at that time, when they returned from their mission they testified that they cast out demons.

> After these things the Lord appointed seventy
> others also, and sent them two by two before His

face into every city and place where He Himself was about to go. Then He said to them, "The harvest truly is great, but the laborers are few; therefore, pray the Lord of the harvest to send out laborers into His harvest. Go your way; behold, I send you out as lambs among wolves. Carry neither money bag, knapsack, nor sandals; and greet no one along the road. But whatever house you enter, first say, 'Peace to this house.' And if a son of peace is there, your peace will rest on it; if not, it will return to you. And remain in the same house, eating and drinking such things as they give, for the laborer is worthy of his wages. Do not go from house to house. Whatever city you enter, and they receive you, eat such things as are set before you. And heal the sick there, and say to them, 'The kingdom of God has come near to you." (Luke 10:1–9)

Luke 10:17–21 further explains,

Then the seventy returned with joy, saying, "Lord, even the demons are subject to us in your name." And He said to them, "I saw Satan fall like lightning from heaven. Behold, I give you the authority to trample on serpents and scorpions, and over all the power of the enemy, and nothing shall by any means hurt you. Nevertheless, do not rejoice in this, that the spirits are subject to you, but rather rejoice because your names are written in heaven." In that hour Jesus rejoiced

in the Spirit and said, "I thank you, Father, Lord
of heaven and earth, that you have hidden these
things from the wise and prudent and revealed
them to babes, even so, Father, for so it seemed
good in your sight."

We see how diseases were healed and demons were cast
out by the disciples. To cast out demons and heal diseases, the
believers had to have the anointing power of the Holy Spirit.
This is a further proof that the Holy Spirit power, which is the
believers personal spiritual power (anointing), is a manifestation
or evidence of being filled or baptized with the Holy Spirit even
though they had not spoken in tongues yet.

What does this mean? It means there is a time and a season for
everything in the plan of God. The day of Pentecost was God's
time and season to fulfill the prophecy of Joel 2:28–29 and Isaiah
28:11–12.

Again Jesus sent the twelve with power. He gave them
power (anointing) and authority over all demons and to cure
diseases, as seen in Luke 10. It is also true that the prophets of
the Old Testament days did not speak in tongues yet performed
supernatural miracles because they were all filled with the
Holy Spirit.

Take note that all miracles, signs, and wonders from the
beginning of creation to now, which are attributed to God, are
all done by the Holy Spirit. Remember, God is Spirit, and to
differentiate from evil spirits is why the Spirit of God is properly
referred to as *Holy Spirit*. The Holy Spirit is God.

Beloved, this is not an exhaustive dissertation on the Holy
Spirit. Nevertheless, I believe that by the grace of God you
have understood a little bit more about the length, breath,

width, and height concerning the Holy Spirit. Just remember one thing: anyone filled with Holy Spirit will, in time, come to know the truth, because the Holy Spirit is the one who leads us into all truth.

John 16:13 states, "However, when He, the Spirit of truth, has come, He will guide you into all truth."

First Corinthians 14:39–40: "Therefore, brethren, desire earnestly to prophesy, and do not forbid to speak with tongues. Let all things be done decently and in order."

Love

There is a danger to speak in tongues without love. According to 1 Corinthians 13:1–2, "Though I speak with the tongues of men and of angels, but have not love, I have become as sounding brass or a clanging cymbal. And though I have the gift of prophecy, and understand all mysteries and all knowledge, and though I have all faith, so that I could remove mountains, but have not love I am nothing."

You can speak in tongues privately in your prayers or praises because those who speak unknown tongues speak mysteries unto God and edify themselves, as revealed in 1 Corinthians 14:1–5: "Pursue love, and desire spiritual gifts, but especially that you may prophesy. For he who speaks in a tongue does not speak to men but to God, for no one understands him; however, in the spirit he speaks mysteries. But he who prophesies speaks edification and exhortation and comfort to men. He who speaks in tongues edifies himself, but he who prophesies edifies the church. I wish you all spoke with tongues but even more that you prophesied; for he who prophesies is greater than he who speaks with tongues, unless indeed he interprets, that the church may receive edification."

I give God thanks for whichever type of gift of tongues the Holy Spirit has given you. Use it for edification of the church, self-edification, and to the praise and glory of God, and remember you are commanded to pursue love as seen above. Be filled with the Spirit. Receive your anointing and be on fire for Jesus.

May the Lord continue to increase your knowledge, for he that increases knowledge increases power, and it is not good for a child of God to be without knowledge. As it is written in Proverbs 24:5: "A man of knowledge increases strength."

The Lord be with you and bless you always and use you as a vessel of honor in the name of the Lord Jesus, our Messiah.

CHAPTER 12

Blaspheme Not, Grieve Not, Quench Not

Elsewhere in this book it has been revealed that the Holy Spirit is the Spirit of Jesus Christ, the Spirit of God, and that the Holy Spirit is God. The apparent lack of personal relationship with the Holy Spirit has caused a lot of people to sin against the Holy Spirit. The Holy Spirit has feelings, emotions, character, and integrity and cares about respect, honor, and dignity. Unholy and irreverent behavior toward the Holy Spirit is also rampant in God's own church and among God's own believers. I believe that believers' destruction in the kingdom of God is classically due to lack of knowledge in the awesome fear of God.

So let me share some more knowledge and understanding with you. Again, for clarity, the author has classified what you must *not* do against the Holy Spirit into eight categories, from the Old Testament to the New Testament.

Rebel not against the Holy Spirit of God

Webster defines the word *rebel* as "to oppose or disobey one in authority or control; to renounce and resist by force the authority of one's government; to act in or show opposition or disobedience; to feel or exhibit anger or revulsion."

One who behaves like this is referred to as a "rebel." Rebellion comes out of the pit of indiscipline and idolatry. Satan is the chief rebel. He rebelled against God in heaven and was cast out of the presence of the Most High God in heaven. Here on earth, in the church, family, place of employment and among every group of people, Satan is unfailingly the source of all rebellion against the will of God, the Son of God, and the Holy Spirit of God. The Lucifer spirit is the same as the Judas Iscariot spirit and is the same spirit of rebellion and indiscipline that rages through our society these last days.

It is important to note that rebellion is the same as disobedience as seen in 1 Samuel 15:22–23: "Then Samuel said: 'Has the Lord as great delight in burnt offerings and sacrifices, as in obeying the voice of the Lord? Behold, to obey is better than sacrifice, and to heed than the fat of rams. For rebellion is as the sin of witchcraft, and stubbornness is as iniquity and idolatry. Because you have rejected the word of the Lord, He also has rejected you from being king.'"

In Isaiah 63:9–10, the Scriptures speaking of the congregation of Israel reveal: "In all their affliction, He was afflicted, and the Angel of His presence saved them; In His love and in His pity, He redeemed them and He bore them and carried them all the days of old. But they rebelled and grieved His Holy Spirit so He turned Himself against them as an enemy, and He fought against them."

During the time of affliction, when you were down and out and nothing could help you during trials and tribulation, God had pity and compassion, and redeemed and bought you through Jesus Christ. Now life is good and prosperous so you rebel against God. This was the grieving attitude of the Children of Israel after God delivered them from Egypt and when they started to prosper in Canaan. The same is the attitude of many believers today that the Lord has healed, delivered and set free. They rebel against God and grieve the Holy Spirit. Be careful; just like God destroyed them in the wilderness, because of their rebellion, you can bring the curse of God and destruction to your soul and life. Our God is also a consuming fire. Be very careful that the Devil does not deceive you to rebel against your maker.

Korah, Dathan, and Abiram Rebelled against Prophet Moses and Perished

The case of Korah, Dathan and Abiram is a clear example of rebellion against the Holy Spirit in Moses. The end result was also clear, precise, and disastrous for the rebels.

We see in Numbers 16:31–35,

> Then it came to pass, as he finished speaking all these words, that the ground split apart under them, and the earth opened its mouth and swallowed them up, with their household and all the men with Korah, with all their goods. So they and all those with them went down alive into the pit; the earth closed over them, and they perished from among the congregation. Then all Israel who were around them fled at their cry, for they said, "Lest the earth swallow us up also!" And a fire came out from the Lord and consumed the two hundred and fifty men who were offering incense.

Take note that to rebel against God is sin, which brings God's anger and judgment on you swiftly.

Israel Rebelled against God in the Wilderness and Brought Curses and Death upon Themselves

To rebel against God means you don't believe God and do not trust God, a condition passionately described in Psalm 78:17–22: "But they sinned even more against Him by rebelling against the Most High in the wilderness. And they tested God in their heart by asking for the food of their fancy. Yes, they spoke against God: they said, 'Can God prepare a table in the wilderness? Behold, He struck the rock, so that the waters gushed out, and the streams overflowed. Can He give bread also? Can He provide meat for His people?' Therefore the Lord heard this and was furious; so a fire was kindled against Jacob, and anger also came up against Israel, because they did not believe in God, and did not trust in His salvation."

Believer, God has saved you, washed your sins away with the blood of His only begotten Son, Jesus, and filled you with His Holy Spirit. Do not rebel against your savior. You will only bring calamity and curses upon yourself as is revealed in Colossian 3:2–6; let us heed what the apostle Paul counsels in Colossians 3:17, 23–24:

Colossians 3:17: "And whatever you do in word or deed, do all in the name of the Lord Jesus, giving thanks to God the Father through Him."

Colossians 3:23–24: "And whatever you do, do it heartily, as to the Lord and not to men, knowing that from the Lord you will receive the reward of the inheritance; for you serve the Lord Christ."

Blaspheme not against the Holy Spirit of God

Blasphemeo is the Greek verb for "to blaspheme." Blaspheme is defined as "to speak of or address with irreverence; to slander, to speak evil of, to revile, abuse or debase one who is divine and that which is sacred or holy."

Any such utterance, contemptuous of God, is referred to as blasphemy, and anyone who blasphemes is a blasphemer. In Vine's expository Dictionary of Old and New Testament words, W. E. Vine, says the word blasphemy is practically confined to speech defamatory of the divine Majesty.

The Lord Jesus Christ reveals the fearful judgment that awaits the blasphemer in Matthew 12:31–32: "Therefore I say to you, every sin and blasphemy will be forgiven men, but the blasphemy against the Spirit will not be forgiven men. Anyone who speaks a word against the Son of Man, it will be forgiven him; but whoever speaks against the Holy Spirit, it will not be forgiven him, either in this age or in the age to come."

Life or death, indeed, is in the mouth. Here the Lord Jesus declares that any blasphemy against the Holy Spirit is a sin, which will not be forgiven now and in the age to come. Blasphemy against the Holy Spirit is known as the unpardonable sin for anybody, believers and unbelievers. God is no respecter of persons. Blasphemy is also known as sin unto death (eternal death).

So, believer, guard your tongue, your mouth, your mind, and your heart from this sin. Remember that if you blaspheme against the Holy Spirit, you will lose your salvation, not to mention your anointing, and frankly, you are eternally doomed and there is no repentance or forgiveness, ever.

The case of the Pharisees blasphemy against the Holy Spirit of the Lord Jesus in Matthew 12:22–37 is worth studying very carefully. Both the believer and unbeliever have opportunity here to pay heed to apostle Paul's counsel in Colossian 3:8: "Now, you must also put off all these; anger, wrath, malice, blasphemy, filthy language out of your mouth."

Lie not to the Holy Spirit of God

To lie is to make an untrue statement with intent to deceive or create a false or misleading impression. Anyone who engages in making untruthful statements is regarded as a liar.

To lie to the Holy Spirit is to lie to God. Therefore, lying to a Holy Spirit baptized and anointed servant of God is the same as lying to God. Let me share a few examples of the catastrophic consequences of lying to God or lying to the Holy Spirit in the servant of God or a believer.

Cain lies to God and brings severe curse on himself in Genesis 4:8–11: "Now Cain talked with Abel his brother; and it came to pass, when they were in the field, that Cain rose against Abel his brother and killed him. Then the Lord said to Cain, 'Where is Abel your brother?' and he said, 'I do not know. Am I my brother's keeper?' And He said, 'What have you done? The voice of your brother's blood cries out to me from the ground. So now you are cursed from the earth, which has opened its mouth to receive your brother's blood from your hand.'" Here, Cain erroneously thought God would not know the mortal sin he had committed. Cain and everybody ought to know that God is omniscient and that the eyes of the Lord are everywhere, looking at the good and the bad.

Gehazi lied to prophet Elisha and brought a curse on himself in 2 Kings 5:20–27:

But Gehazi, the servant of Elisha the man of God, said, "Look, my master has spared Naaman this Syrian, while not receiving from his hands what he brought; but as the Lord lives, I will run after him and take something from him." So Gehazi pursued Naaman. When Naaman saw him running after him, he got down from the chariot to meet him, and said, "It is all well?" And he said, "All is well, my master has sent me, saying, indeed, just now two young men of the sons of the prophets have come to me from the mountains of Ephraim. Please give them a talent of silver and two changes of garments." So Naaman said, "Please, take two talents," and he urged him, and bound two talents of silver in two bags, with two changes of garments, and handed them to two of his servants and they carried them on ahead of him. When he came to the citadel, he took them from their hand and stored them away in the house; then he let the men go, and they departed. Now he went in and stood before his master. And Elisha said to him, "Where did you go, Gehazi?" and he said, "Your servant did not go anywhere." Then he said to him, "Did not my heart go with you when the man turned back from his chariot to meet you? Is it time to receive money and to receive clothing, olive groves and vineyard, sheep and oxen, male and female servant? "Therefore the leprosy of Naaman shall cling to you and your descendants forever." And he went out from his presence leprous, as white as snow.

In this case, Gehazi erroneously thought that he was talking to a mere man Elisha.

The truth is, prophet Elisha was filled with the Holy Spirit of God, who indwelt the prophet at all times even to the grave. The Holy Spirit of God in the prophet is God and knows all things and reveals all things. So when Gehazi lied to the prophet Elisha, he did not lie to man but to the Spirit of God in Elisha. Consequently, Gehazi was cursed by God without fail.

King Saul lied to prophet Samuel and brought a curse to himself in 1 Samuel 15:13–14, 22–23.

1 Samuel 15:13–14: "Then Samuel went to Saul, and Saul said to him, 'Blessed are you of the Lord! I have performed the commandment of the Lord.' But Samuel said, 'What then is this bleating of the sheep in my ears, and the lowing of the oxen which I hear?'"

1 Samuel 15:22–23: "Then Samuel said, 'Has the Lord as great delight in burnt offerings and sacrifices, as in obeying the voice of the Lord? Behold, to obey is better than sacrifice, and heed than the fat of rams for rebellion is as the sin of witchcraft, and stubbornness is as iniquity and idolatry. Because you have rejected the word of the Lord, He also has rejected you from being king.'"

It is evident that King Saul also overlooked the Holy Spirit of God in prophet Samuel and went ahead to lie to the Spirit of the Lord. The king was cursed because God is no respecter of persons. He lost his kingdom, the Holy Spirit, his anointing, and an evil spirit troubled him.

Ananias and his wife, Sapphira, lied to apostle Peter and brought a fatal curse on themselves in Acts 5:1-5, 7-10.

Acts 5:1–5: "But a certain man named Ananias, with Sapphira, his wife, sold a possession and he kept back a part of the proceeds, his wife also being aware of it, and brought a certain part and laid it at the apostles' feet, but Peter said, 'Ananias, why has Satan filled your heart to lie to the Holy Spirit and keep back part of the price of the land for yourself? While it remained, was it not your own? And after it was sold, was it not in your own control? Why have you conceived this thing in your heart? You have not lied to men but to God?' Then Ananias, hearing these words, fell down and breathed his last. So great fear came upon all those who heard these things."

Acts 5:7–10: "Now it was about three hours later when his wife came in, not knowing what had happened. And Peter answered her, 'Tell me whether you sold the land for so much?' and she said, 'Yes, for so much.' Then Peter said to her, 'How is it that you have agreed together to test the Spirit of the Lord? Look, the feet of those who have buried your husband are at the door, and they will carry you out.' Then immediately she fell down at his feet and breathed her last. And the young men came in and found her dead, and carrying her out, buried her by her husband."

The deception of Satan is to deceive you into thinking that the servant of God is only human and will not know the truth. This is unbelief and lack of knowledge which nevertheless, will bring curses and fatal destruction to any person lying to the Holy Spirit of God in the servant of God.

It is evident that to lie to the Holy Spirit of God is to assume that God will not know the truth. It is a terrible fatal presumption that can bring eternal judgment on you. The truth is, God is sovereign, omniscient, omnipotent, and is the final judge of all minds, heart, and intents.

Hebrews 4:13 emphatically declares, "There is no creature hidden from His sight, but all things are naked and open to the eyes of Him to whom we must give account."

Believer, fear God and receive counsel from apostle Paul, which he declared in Colossians 3:9 "Do not lie to one another, since you have put off the old man with his deeds." If you are commanded not to *lie* to one another, God is greater than any one of us. Therefore, do not lie to God but fear God.

Resist not the Holy Spirit of God

To resist is to exert yourself to counteract or defeat, says Webster. It is to withstand and oppose the force or power of someone or something.

Elymas resisted apostle Paul and brought a curse on himself, according to Acts 13:6–11.

> Now when they had gone through the island to Paphos, they found a certain sorcerer, a false prophet, a Jew whose name was Bar-Jesus, who was with the proconsul, Sergius Paulus, an intelligent man, this man called for Barnabas and Saul and sought to hear the word of God. But Elymas the sorcerer (for so his name is translated) withstood them, seeking to turn the proconsul away from the faith. Then Saul, who also is called Paul, filled with the Holy Spirit, looked intently at him and said, "O full of all deceit and all fraud, you son of the Devil, you enemy of all righteousness, will you not cease perverting the straight ways of the Lord? And now, indeed, the hand of the Lord is upon you, and you shall be blind, not seeing the sun for a time." And immediately a dark mist fell on him, and he went around seeking someone to lead him by the hand.

Elymas the sorcerer tried to withstand the Holy Spirit in apostle Paul. He thought Paul was an ordinary man and therefore opposed and attempted to overpower him by his evil spirit of sorcery or witchcraft. His error in resisting the Holy Spirit in the apostle caused a divine judgment, which resulted in blinding the evil sorcerer.

Believers are cautioned never to resist or withstand the power (anointing) of God in the servant of our Lord. We are to resist the Devil, not the Holy Spirit. To resist the Holy Spirit is to counteract and withstand the power of God. It seems to me that only a child of perdition, reprobate minds, and the absolute ignorant person resists the Holy Spirit of God. Be reminded that multitudes were delivered from the claws of Pharaoh and out of Egypt. But when the children of Israel resisted, rebelled, and murmured against God in the wilderness, most were destroyed, and very few of the original Jews who came out of Egypt possessed the Promised Land.

In Acts 7:51, because Israel continued to resist the Holy Spirit, they are called stiff-necked, uncircumcised in heart and in ears, characteristics which lead straight to hardships, trials and tribulations. Believer, would you like to be called stiff-necked (stubborn, self-willed, disobedient, and blind), uncircumcised in heart and ears? I don't think so. I would rather be on my way to heaven than to hell. There are many believers who block their own blessings from God (stop blaming the Devil for everything) because you are resisting the Holy Spirit (your Helper), and you may not even know it. There are those who are in denial. The Holy Spirit is here to be your eternal companion (the unseen God) and bring God's blessings upon you until there is no room to receive it.

Do not resist Him but open the door of your heart and let Him in to bless you. God is looking for someone to bless, and you are the chosen one.

Grieve not the Holy Spirit of God

The Greek word *lupeomia,* or *Lupeo,* means to cause to grieve or to make sorrowful. This is an inward grief, which goes to the level of the soul, mind, and heart. Webster defines grief as to cause to suffer distress. It also means to feel sorrow.

This is why the Lord Jesus, who was acquainted with grief, is rightfully called "a man of sorrow."

People of the first world grieved God and brought destruction upon the world, according to Genesis 6:5–7. "Then the Lord saw that the wickedness of man was great in the earth, and that every intent and thoughts of his heart was only evil continually and the Lord was sorry that He had made man on the earth, and He was grieved in His heart. So the Lord said, 'I will destroy man whom I have created from the face of the earth, both man and beast, creeping thing and birds of the air, for I am sorry that I have made them.'"

A close examination of these terrifying verses reveals that first, man was and still is wicked. The intent and thoughts of his heart was and still is continually evil. Indeed, Jeremiah declared in Jeremiah 17:9 "that the heart is deceitful above all things and desperately wicked." Second, this wickedness and evil ways of man grieved God so much so that God decided to destroy man and beast from the face of the earth. Finally, the first global catastrophe came upon man as seen in Genesis 7:23: "So He destroyed all living things which were on the face of the ground: both man and cattle, creeping things and bird of the air. They were destroyed from the earth. Only Noah and those who were with him in the ark remained alive."

Israel Grieved God in the Wilderness and Brought Destruction on Themselves

Psalm 78:40: "How often they provoked Him in the wilderness and grieved Him in the desert."

Psalm 78:59 states that as a result of all the things Israel did to grieve God, He abhorred them and was so furious that in Psalm 78: 62–63, "He also gave His people over to the sword and was furious with His inheritance. The fire consumed their young men and their maidens were not given in marriage."

For example, if you can't find a spouse, it just maybe that the curse of God is upon you for grieving His Spirit. Increase your knowledge about the terrible consequences of grieving the Spirit of God and by avoiding it, you could cause the hand of God to release your prosperity, victory, anointing, and your heart's desires.

Psalm 95:10–11: "For forty years I was grieved with that generation, and said, "it is a people who go astray in their hearts, and they do not know my ways. So I swore in my wrath, they shall not enter my rest."

Again it is evident that when you grieve the Holy Spirit of God you invoke the wrath of God on yourself.

The heathen Is Destroyed for Grieving God

God also destroys heathens when they grieve Him. The longsuffering of God is to allow the heathen a chance to believe in order to be saved. But if the unbeliever grieves God just like

Pharaoh hardened his heart against God in Egypt, Psalm 78:49 reveals what happened to him and the Egyptians: "He cast on them the fierceness of His anger, wrath, indignation, and trouble by sending angels of destruction among them."

The consequences of grieving the Spirit of God is so catastrophic that the apostle Paul warns sternly in Ephesians 4:30: "Do not grieve the Holy Spirit of God by whom you were sealed for the day of redemption." Some of the things that grieve God include, sin, anger, wrath, malice, blasphemy, filthy language, unbelief, bitterness, clamor, and evil speaking.

Indeed, to grieve or not to grieve the Holy Spirit of God is not an option. You are commanded *not* to grieve the Holy Spirit of God. If you know God and love God, obey His commands and you shall exceedingly abundantly be blessed. God desires to prosper you, but you could bring curses and destruction to yourself if you grieve His Spirit. Remember, grieve not the Holy Spirit of God.

Provoke not the Holy Spirit of God to Anger

To provoke means to incite to anger or to stir up purposely or to provide the needed stimulus. It also means to agitate or vex and displease the Spirit or soul of another.

The act or end product is provocation. The prophecy of 2 Timothy 3:1–5 is being fulfilled in these last days. Believer, we are living in the days of provocation. Daily in our homes, wives provoke husbands and husbands provoke wives, parents provoke children and children provoke parents. Family feuding has become rampant and (sadly) popular because television has turned it into reality TV. Employers provoke employees and employees provoke employers. The list is endless.

On a daily basis, we are bombarded with so much active provocation that people provoke others to anger as if it is normal. The rampant and raging pugnacious spirits, wars, homicide, divorce, and paranoia that exist in these days are rooted in active provocation viciously propagated and managed by our enemy, Lucifer, the Devil, his legions of evil spirits, and the Devil's advocates, who have sneaked into churches to deceive, provoke, manipulate people, and cause major confusion among believers. Identify them and cast them out.

Romans 16:17–18: "Now I urge you, brethren note those who cause divisions and offenses, contrary to the doctrine which you learned, and avoid them. For those who are such do not serve our Lord Jesus Christ, but their own belly, and with smooth words and flattering speech deceive the hearts of the simple."

Second John 1:10–11: "If anyone comes to you and does not bring this doctrine, do not receive him into your house nor greet him; for he who greets him shares in his evil deeds."

Believers also perpetrate this sin of provocation when we do not abide in the word of God as commanded in

John 15:7: "If you abide in me, and my words abide in you, you will ask what you desire, and it shall be done for you."

One day, after more than four hundred years of suffering in Egypt, the great I AM responded to the prayers of suffering Jewish slaves in Egypt. The prophet Moses was sent to deliver the children of Israel from the tyrannical hands of Pharaoh. God did miracles by the hands of Moses to accomplish their deliverance.

Nevertheless, the people became ungrateful, unthankful and constantly provoked God (Holy Spirit in Moses) unto anger. (Notice that when people are going through very difficult times, they are humble, even obedient.)

As soon as their yokes are destroyed and their curses broken, their pride, egos, and evil behavior show up to bite, provoke, and turn against their savior. I have seen this evil in many ministries. Like pigs, spoken of by the Lord Jesus, they turn around to bite you, as revealed in Matthew 7:6: "Do not give what is holy to the dogs; nor cast your pearls before swine, lest they trample them under their feet, and turn and tear you in pieces."

Numbers 14:11–12 states, "And the Lord said to Moses, 'How long will these people reject me? And how long will they not believe me, with all the signs which I have performed among them? I will strike them with the pestilence and disinherit them, and I will make of you a nation greater and mightier than they.'"

God was ready to destroy them because they provoked Him to anger. Indeed Psalm 78 has a litany of what God did for Israel but verse 56 announces, "Yet they tested and provoked the Most High God, and did not keep His testimonies." Verse 57 states, "But turned back and acted unfaithfully like their fathers; they were turned aside like a deceitful bow." Psalm 78:58: "For they provoked Him to anger with their high places, and moved Him to jealously with their graven images." "The fire consumed their young men, And their maidens were not given in marriage."(Psalm 78:63)

Beloved, God destroyed everyone of them that provoked the Spirit of God unto anger and our God of yesterday is the same today as declared in Malachi 3:6, "I am the Lord, I change not."

Proverbs 20:2 reveals, "The wrath of a king is like the roaring of a lion; whoever provokes him to anger sins against his own life."

Let us be wise and provoke not, but ever praise His Holy name for His goodness, mercy, and grace. Remember that He is the King of Kings, so provoke not the King and you shall be blessed.

Insult not the Holy Spirit of God

To insult is to treat a thing or a person with insolence, indignity or contempt. One who insults always behaves with pride and arrogance.

Therefore, to insult the Holy Spirit of God is to demonstrate pride and arrogance before the creator of heaven and earth and all who are in it. How can mortal man treat the omnipotent God with contempt? Yet Hebrew 10:29 reveals that people behave always in a way as to insult God. "Of how much worse punishment, do you suppose will he be thought worthy who has trampled the Son of God underfoot, counted the blood of the covenant by which he was sanctified a common thing, and insulted the Spirit of grace?"

Pride, egos, and blissful ignorance are the underlying factors that cause people to insult the Spirit of God. There is a definite punishment from God against anyone who insults the Spirit of God. Proverbs 6:17 declares that a proud look is one of the seven abominations that God hates. I believe God will not bless you when He hates you.

God wants to lift you up, bless and prosper you, and all you have to do is to humble yourself in the sight of the Lord. Be careful that you never insult the Holy Spirit of God in your speech, actions, in your thoughts, in your mind and heart and you shall be blessed with the peace, prosperity, and salvation of God.

Quench not the Holy Spirit of God

Webster defines quench as to put out, extinguish, put out light or fire, to cool or smother. First Thessalonians 5:19 says, "Do not put out the Spirit's Fire" (NIV). "Do not quench the Spirit" (The New King James Version). There are several ways to look at this Scripture.

a. To quench or not to quench the Holy Spirit of God is not an option for the believer.
b. It is a command to the believer *not* to quench the Spirit.
c. To put out the Spirit's fire may also be interpreted as being lukewarm.

Revelation 3:15–16 warns the church of Laodicea, "You are neither cold nor hot; I could wish you were cold or hot. So then, because you are lukewarm and neither cold nor hot, I will spew you out of my mouth."

This church needed a revival to rekindle and set ablaze the fire of the Holy Spirit.

d. To quench the Spirit could also mean to suppress the manifestations of the gifts of the Holy Spirit in the church. In this case, the church can come back to life by stirring up the gifts that the Holy Spirit has imparted to the individuals in the church.

The bishop or pastor could stir up his own gifts to stir up the entire church. Where the Spirit is quenched, there is no manifestation of Holy Spirit anointing power and only a form of godliness exist. Of such is a "dead church."

e. What water is to fire, so is sin to the Holy Spirit of God. The psalmist declares you are a God that cannot live with sin. Thus sin can literally put out the Holy Spirit in you. In this case, to quench the Holy Spirit is to cause God to remove your light or the Holy Spirit from you. It was for this possibility that King David prayed to God in Psalm 51:11: "Do not cast me away from your presence and do not take your Holy Spirit from me."

Remember that when the Holy Spirit of God departed from King Saul, the Bible reveals that an evil spirit began to trouble him. Depart from sin and the Holy Spirit will not depart from you.

f. The believer is the light of the world because of the Holy Spirit and the word of God. Of course the chief light of the world is the Lord Jesus Christ. But the believer is commanded to let your light shine, therefore, to quench the Holy Spirit is to extinguish, put out or at the least dim your light. If you focus on letting your Holy Spirit light shine before all men that they may see your good works; there will be no opportunity to quench the Spirit.

It is evident that many people, not excluding believers, either do not know nor care or forget what God has decreed in 1 Chronicles 16:21–22 referenced in Psalm 105: 14–15: "He permitted no one to do them wrong; yes, He reproved kings for their sakes, saying, 'Do not touch my anointed one and do my prophets no harm.'"

God certainly has commanded that no one, great or small shall touch nor do any harm to any of His anointed ones, servants and prophets by word or deed.

In Isaiah 55:17, Jehovah clarified the protection and power (authority) of His servants saying, "No weapon formed against you shall prosper and every tongue which rise against you in judgment you shall condemn. This is the heritage of the servant of the Lord and their righteousness is from me, says the Lord."

g. First John 1:5 reveals "God is light and in Him is no darkness at all." Here, it is evident that to quench the Holy Spirit of God is to move out of God's marvelous light into darkness.

This is the case when a believer backslides and goes back into the works of the old person and the world. To overcome this, the believer needs to put on the new person and allow old things to pass away.

It's time for the latter rain. God is pouring out His Holy Spirit on all flesh. Receive your Holy Spirit baptism and stir up the gifts and let the fire of the Holy Spirit burn in you. Yes, be on fire for Jesus. Be zealous and always abound in the work of the Lord and be comforted that your labor is never in vain in the Lord.

Resist not, lie not, blaspheme not, grieve not, and sin not against the Holy Spirit of God, and the peace of God that passes all understanding shall take care of your mind and heart with exceedingly abundant blessing from God to you.

Epilogue

The Holy Spirit is the Spirit of love. Earnestly desire the best gifts but now abide faith, hope, and love. The greatest of these is love. First Corinthians 13:13 says the Holy Spirit is the Spirit of God and He is God. God is love. I pray therefore that even as the God of love has shed His love in us and given us His Spirit of love, that in all things in word or in deed we do it with love in our hearts. There are different kinds of love, let the supernatural agape love of God supersede all other types of love in all your relations with the brethren.

How beautiful it is for brethren to dwell together in *unity*. The unity of the Spirit of love brings peace, progress and prosperity to the children of God. God loves us so let us love one another with the Spirit of love.

If we love one another as commanded by the Lord, the world we seek to convert will know that the believers are true disciples of the Lord Jesus and great power will be given to us as in the days of old.

With abundant love in your heart, soul, and spirit, pick up your sword to do damage to the kingdom of Satan. Put on the whole armor of God because you are a true soldier in the army of God. You are an overcomer and by your faith in Jesus Christ, you have already overcome the world. You can be the best in anything you do for the Lord because you can do all things through Christ who is the true source of your inexhaustible strength. When the time comes for you to wait on the Lord, just wait because God is simply preparing you with new strength to run and not get tired and mount you up with new wings to fly like the eagle that you are. Contend for the faith that was once given to the saints of old.

There is a time and season for everything. This is your time to rise up in the power of His might and work the works of God in the name of Jesus. Those who believe in Jesus and the work He did you shall do, and greater works you shall do. All the anointing you need is already in you, and greater is He that is in you than anything you'll encounter.

So, soldier and child of God, get up and be about your Father's business. Yes, be on fire for Jesus. Amen.

About the Author

Dr. Emmanuel Osei-Acheampong has received a divine supernatural calling to preach and teach the word of God with power and revelation knowledge.

He is a gifted man with a true apostolic and prophetic calling on his life. Dr. Osei-Acheampong is dedicated to training, equipping, imparting, and activating the gifts of the Holy Spirit in ministers and believers to reach nations with the supernatural power and revelation knowledge of our Lord and Savior Jesus Christ.

Dr. Osei-Acheampong is the founder of the Jesus Commission Ministries, Inc. in the United States of America and Africa.

This book is to free your mind, body, and soul from putting the almighty God in a box of rules and regulations of creeds, dogmas, religion, articles and statements of faith, affirmations, denominations, organizational sectarianism, and name-brand ministries with all its paraphernalia.

Dr. Emmanuel Osei-Acheampong has received a divine supernatural calling to preach and teach the Word of God with power and revelation knowledge. Dr. Osei-Acheampong is dedicated to training, equipping, imparting, and activating the gifts of the Holy Spirit in ministers and believers to reach nations with the supernatural power and revelation knowledge of our Lord and Savior Jesus Christ. Dr. Osei-Acheampong is the founder of the Jesus Commission Ministries, Inc. in the United States of America and Africa.

To get more knowledge and understanding about the Holy Spirit, please connect now to the author at uccnow.org

WESTBOW
PRESS
A DIVISION OF THOMAS NELSON
& ZONDERVAN